SOLDIER STORIES

SOLDIER
STORIES

TRUE TALES OF COURAGE, HONOR, AND

SACRIFICE FROM THE FRONTLINES

JOE WHEELER

W PUBLISHING GROUP
A Division of Thomas Nelson Publishers
Since 1798

www.wpublishinggroup.com

SOLDIER STORIES
Copyright © 2006 Joe L. Wheeler

Published by W Publishing Group, a Division of Thomas Nelson, Inc., P.O. Box 141000, Nashville, Tennessee, 37214.

W Publishing Group books may be purchased in bulk for educational, business, fundraising, or sales promotional use. For information, please e-mail SpecialMarkets@ThomasNelson.com.

All Scripture quotations, unless otherwise indicated, are taken from the The King James Version of the Bible (KJV).

Editorial Staff: Greg Daniel, acquisition editor, and Thom Chittom, managing editor

Cover Design: Designpoint

Page Design: Lori Lynch, Book & Graphic Design, Nashville, TN

Library of Congress Cataloging-in-Publication Data

Wheeler, Joe L., 1936-
  Soldier stories / by Joe Wheeler.
    p. cm.
  ISBN-10: 0-8499-1217-2
  ISBN-13: 978-0-8499-1217-7
  1. Soldiers—Biography. 2. Soldiers—United States—Biography. 3. Military history, Modern—20th century. 4. Military history, Modern—20th century. 5. United States—History, Military—20th century. 6. United States—History, Military—21st century. I. Title.
  U51.W458 2006
  355.0092'273--dc22

                          2006024230

Printed in the United States of America
06 07 08 09 10 RRD 5 4 3 2 1

★ ★ ★

She designed our website, and, day in and day out, responds to all those who log in seeking information about our books, about the life and times of Zane and Dolly Grey, or about the books and stories Grey wrote.

When I'm slow at responding to a query, she jogs my memory and asks why it's taking me so long.

Besides all this, she's always been one very wonderful daughter!

Thus it gives me great joy to dedicate *Soldier Stories* to

MICHELLE WHEELER CULMORE

of

ANNAPOLIS, MARYLAND

CONTENTS

IN FLANDERS FIELDS

In Flanders fields
the poppies blow
Between the Crosses,
row on row,
That mark our place;
and in the sky
The larks, still bravely
singing, fly,
Scarce heard amidst
the guns below.

We are the dead.
Short days ago we lived,
felt dawn,
saw sunset glow,
Loved and were loved,
and now we lie
In Flanders fields.

Take up our quarrel
with the foe,
To you from failing hands,
we throw the Torch—
be yours to hold it high;
If ye break faith
with us who die,
We shall not sleep,
though poppies grow
In Flanders fields.

Some years ago in an antique shop, I stumbled on what is today one of my most cherished possessions, this poem in a battered frame with a backing of crumbling brown paper. It clearly dates back to World War I and was originally hung, most likely, on the wall of a home that had already experienced loss. It now hangs in my office where I can see it every day.

Without question, "We Shall Not Sleep" (better known as "In Flanders Fields") is the best known and most loved of all poems written during what contemporaries called "The Great War." These words are handwritten in ink on the crumbling paper that backs the frame: "This poem, 'We Shall Not Sleep,' by Lt. Col. Dr. John McCrae, Montreal, Canada, was written while the second Battle of Ypres was in progress. The Author's body now lies in Flanders Fields."

Canada, too, saw two generations of its brightest and best fight and die on that soil.

★
★ NOTHING IN LIFE IS SO
★ EXHILARATING AS TO BE SHOT
   AT WITHOUT RESULT.

                   —WINSTON CHURCHILL

INTRODUCTION:
THE FASCINATION OF WAR

JOSEPH LEININGER WHEELER

I t is well that war is so terrible, or we should get too fond of it." So mused General Robert E. Lee, as he watched his troops repel a Federal Cavalry charge at Fredericksburg.

As for history itself, what is it but the story of exciting wars broken up by boring stretches of peace? One would think that as terrible as the reality of war is, with the deaths of loved ones and the returning of veterans who are incapacitated for life, it would be extremely difficult to psych up the populace for another one.

"Not so!" maintained H. L. Mencken, perhaps the most cynical of all our folk philosophers: "War survives simply because so many people enjoy it. . . . The truth is that what the human race really finds it hard to endure is peace. It can stand the dull monotony for ten years, twenty years and even thirty years, but then it begins to fume and lather, and presently we are in the midst of another major war and enjoying its incomparable exhilarations."

Mencken also points out that in history, as illogical as it may appear, the thoughtful earnest leaders who try to keep us out of wars are lucky to avoid being discredited for taking such an unpopular stand: War is, "to at least nine people out of ten, the supreme circus of circuses, the show beyond compare. It is Hollywood multiplied by ten thousand. It combines all the excitement of a bullfight, a revival, a train wreck, and a lynching."

Bertrand Russell concurred: "I discovered to my amazement that average men and women were delighted at the prospects of war. I had fondly imagined what most pacifists contended: that wars were forced upon a reluctant population by despotic and Machiavellian governments."

Chamberlain has been reviled now for four generations. Why? Because he sold out civilization in order to appease Hitler. Of his ilk, the irrepressible Churchill quipped, "An appeaser is one who feeds a crocodile—hoping it will eat him last."

Somewhat surprisingly, there are many who postulate that wars serve useful purposes. In a rather earthy vein, Thomas Jefferson declared: "The tree of liberty must be refreshed from time to time with the blood of patriots and tyrants. It is its natural manure."

Two thousand years ago Juvenal worried more about the debilitating effects of peace than of war: "We are now suffering the evils of a long peace. Luxury, more deadly than war, broods over the city [Rome], and avenges a conquered world." Milton agreed, pointing out in *Paradise Lost* that peace corrupts as much as war lays waste.

And none beat the war drums more enthusiastically than those who have never experienced it themselves. This is plenty reason not to entrust the key decision-making in war to those for whom it is merely a game.

For those who have experienced the full measure of the horrors of war, the messages tend to be radically different. General Sherman, who certainly ought to have known, groused, "I am tired and sick of war. Its glory is all moonshine. It is only those who have neither fired a shot nor heard the shrieks and groans of the wounded who cry aloud for blood, more vengeance, more desolation. War is hell." And famed war correspondent Bill Mauldin put it more succinctly: "Look at the infantryman's eyes and you can tell how much war he has seen."

There was certainly no arrogance in Eisenhower: "Humility must always be the portion of any man who receives acclaim earned in the blood of his followers and the sacrifice of his friends." Indeed, what troubled Ike so much that he reiterated it in his final address to the American people was this: "In the councils of government, we must guard against the acquisition of unwarranted influence, whether sought or unsought, by the military industrial complex. The potential for the disastrous rise of misplaced power exists and will persist." Georges Clemenceau went further and said: "War is too serious a matter to be entrusted to the military."

Franklin went further yet: "There never was a good war or a bad peace."

WAR IN THE TWENTIETH CENTURY

WORLD WAR I

It was in the Balkans where some said the next big war would start. Sure enough, it would be the assassination of Archduke Franz Ferdinand—heir to the throne of the Austro-Hungarian Empire—in Sarajevo, Serbia, on June 28, 1914, that would light the match igniting the first global war.

Luckless France would be the bloodiest battleground of all. In four years' time, with sixty-five million men under arms, nine million men would die, and over twenty-one million soldiers and civilians would be wounded or incapacitated. The United States would stay neutral until 1917, when submarine attacks forced us into the war. Once in France and over one million strong, however, the difference the U.S. made was felt very quickly. Many Americans, especially the aviators, had sneaked into the war early, even if they had to join the French Foreign Legion first.

Many things then happened for the first time in warfare. For example, submarines played a major role. Even though England ruled the seas in 1914, German U-boats sank so many of its ships, and those of its allies, that England was losing steam and facing starvation when America entered the war. Machine guns made battles far deadlier than they'd ever been before. Tanks were introduced for the first time. At the war's beginning, balloons and airplanes were used only for reconnaissance, but by 1915 that changed as pilots began shooting each other down. And then there was that horrific weapon, poisonous gas, which killed silently and without warning. Men fought from trenches day after day, month after month, year after year, frequently being driven back and forth over the same ground; one million two hundred thousand men would die in Verdun alone. In the air it was the age of aces, creating such heroes as the Red Baron, Frank Luke, and Rickenbacker.

Just before the war ended in 1918, in rushed the horrific Spanish Flu pandemic, killing more people than the war itself (somewhere between twenty and forty million people). No one knew what caused it or how to stop it. The flu would later be incorporated into Katherine Anne Porter's *Pale Horse, Pale Rider*.

AFTERMATH OF WORLD WAR I

The war rewrote much of the world's maps, as empires such as Germany, Austria-Hungary, and Russia collapsed. The British Empire had seen an entire generation of its youngest and finest die. Then came savage anti-war poems such as Wilfred Owens's "Dulce Et Decorum Est" and A. E. Houseman's "Is My Team Ploughing." Famine stalked the European continent. The Allies quickly occupied Germany; then turned it over on its back. With its industry and economy in shambles and huge war reparations demanded of it, Germany was so broken, so bitter, so disillusioned, and so desperate, that it was ripe for a demagogue who'd bring it respect and solvency again. Out of World War I came one of the greatest war novels ever written, Erich Maria Remarque's *All Quiet on the Western Front*. This bleak anti-war novel became an instant bestseller. The film won "Best Picture" at the 1930 Oscars and made Remarque an international celebrity. Hitler considered its anti-war message to be so insidious that he had the book banned in Germany, forcing its author into exile. But there were compensations: Remarque thereby got to date Marlene Dietrich and marry Paulette Goddard.

America slipped quickly back into isolation, rejecting even the League of Nations, which broke President Wilson's heart and may have helped to bring on his early death. The war that had begun so idealistically ended in disillusion, cynicism, and despair. It seemed to contemporaries as if the spirit of God had departed from the Earth. Surely they'd just experienced Armageddon.

The Roaring Twenties with its Lost Generation was followed by the Dust Bowl and the terrible worldwide depression of the 1930s. In Europe, by the decade's end, there now ruled three Frankenstein monsters: Mussolini in Italy, Stalin in Russia, and Hitler in Germany. As the world teetered above another abyss, Wilson Mizner, in his 1935 speech to the League of Nations, spoke these sobering words: "It has now become clear to the whole world that each war is the creation of a preceding war and the generation of new, present, or future wars."

Churchill, a year later, warned the world against complacency and appeasement of dictators such as Hitler: "Dictators ride to and fro upon tigers which they dare not dismount. And the tigers are getting hungry."

WORLD WAR II

Each time Hitler swallowed another region or nation, he stopped to see what the world would say. Each time it did nothing to stop him, and he was emboldened to attack another. The world should have known better, for much earlier in his *Mein Kampf,* Hitler had postulated: "Strength lies not in defense but in attack," and "The one means that wins the easiest victory over reason is terror and force."

Finally in 1939, when Hitler's blitzkrieg rolled into Czechoslovakia and Poland, the Allies belatedly mobilized for war—less than twenty-one years after the Armistice Day November 11, 1918. This time it appeared that Germany was unstoppable. Nation after nation fell like toppling dominoes as the blitzkrieg (dive-bombers, bombers, rockets, tanks, machine guns, and infantry) annihilated everything in its path. America determinedly remained neutral. By allying himself with Stalin in the East, Hitler could concentrate all his forces in the West.

According to Robert Stone, "in the sheer quantity of blood spilled, the Second World War was certainly the most horrendous war in history." At least sixty-five million died, fifty million of them civilians! For the first time the military deliberately targeted not just armies but cities, without regard to how many civilians might perish in such indiscriminate attacks. Though Hitler would begin it all, and slaughter six million Jews in infamous concentration camps, the war would end with apocalyptic firestorm bombings of unarmed cities, such as with Dresden and the holocaust of Hiroshima and Nagasaki. Anything much worse would have destroyed civilization itself.

Hitler came within an inch of pulling it off. So rapidly did his armies move that by the end of May 1940, Hitler ruled the land-mass of the European continent all the way from the English Channel to the Balkans and Russia. At its peak the Third Reich's European empire was larger than any other since the days of imperial Rome. The only obstacle left, Hitler wrote off with a laugh, was little England across the channel.

Here Hitler made his biggest mistake: so fast had he rolled through the Low Countries that he had what was left of the entire Allied army (two hundred thousand British and one hundred forty thousand French and Belgians) holed up in the little French seacoast town of Dunkirk. Had Hitler not ordered his pursuing armies elsewhere, it would have all been over. Instead, gaining precious breathing room, Britain pressed every available thing that could float (warships, ferries, fishing boats, pleasure craft) into service. While planes attacked from the air, all but two thousand men made it across to England alive.

But England was still the world's largest empire, its empire and commonwealth covering one-fifth of the world's landmass and one-quarter of its people. It could draw from great nations such as India, Australia, and Canada for its armies and navies. And it still controlled the seas, but German submarines were sinking Allied ships faster than new ones could be constructed.

A great man stood against the ten-million-man army of the Third Reich—the indomitable Winston Churchill, who galvanized an empire by vowing to the House of Commons on June 4, 1940, when the future appeared bleakest: "We shall not flag or fail. We shall go on to the end. We shall fight in France, we shall fight on the seas and oceans, we shall fight with growing confidence and growing strength in the air, we shall defend our island, whatever the cost may be, we shall fight on the beaches, we shall fight on the landing grounds, we shall fight in the fields and in the streets, we shall fight in the hills; we shall never surrender."

The Royal Air Force fought back around the clock as German aircraft filled the skies, bombs fell, and rockets slammed into cities and towns. On August 20, Churchill declared about those intrepid airmen, "Never in the field of human conflict was so much owed by so many to so few."

On the other hand, the world was astonished at how quickly

France fell before the German juggernaut. France's generals excused themselves by prophesying, "In three weeks England will have her neck wrung like a chicken." When that didn't happen, Churchill quipped, "Some chicken; some neck."

Hitler had also written off America, proclaiming that it lacked both the will and the technology to stand up to him. Consequently, he sank our ships with assumed impunity. When Japan assumed the same privilege at Pearl Harbor on December 7, 1941, Roosevelt declared war—and Churchill no longer stood alone. Of course it didn't hurt that Hitler was then hurling nine-tenths of his forces at Russia, desperately needing the Caucasus oil for his war machine. By the time Russia finally stopped the German war machine in the East, Eisenhower was ready to make the greatest amphibious landing in history: the Normandy Invasion. Shortly afterwards war correspondent Ernie Pyle looked up at the sky and saw Allied dive-bombers barreling down from every direction, noting "a gigantic faraway surge of doomlike sound . . . the heavy bombers." Some three thousand planes filled the skies as far as the eye could see. "I've never known a storm, or a machine, or any resolve of man that had about it the aura of such a ghastly relentlessness," Pyle said.

Once again the infantry, by the millions, fought their way across France and into Germany; in the east, Russia closed in as well. America not only fought in Europe, it also fought bloody battles in Africa and the South Pacific against the empire of Japan.

When it was all over at last in 1945, Britain, having given its all (losing the flower of two consecutive generations of young men for the cause of freedom) had been bled dry—and passed the responsibility of defending the western world to America.

THE KOREAN WAR

After World War II the world backed off and left the action to the only remaining superpowers: the United States and the Soviet

Union. While Japan turned to peaceful pursuits, not far away the long-slumbering dragon, China, awakened from its long sleep.

The Atomic Age quickly segued into the Space Age. On October 14, 1947, Chuck Yeager broke the sound barrier. Two years later, Frank Everest climbed to sixty-three thousand feet in the supercharged Bell X-1 rocket plane.

Then without warning, North Korea invaded South Korea on June 25, 1950, and all but swept the occupying forces off the peninsular nation. Douglas MacArthur, supreme commander of the United Nations coalition, staged a daring amphibious landing on the beaches of Inchon, then led his forces northward up the peninsula, both sides sustaining terrible casualties. A year later, victory appeared at hand as the North Korean army was cornered on the border of Communist China. Suddenly, across the Yalu River came over three hundred thousand Chinese soldiers to join the North Korean forces. When MacArthur, in a rage, threatened to bomb China itself, possibly with nuclear bombs, Truman relieved him of command. Two more bloody years followed before Eisenhower, seeing the futility of the war, finally negotiated an armistice in 1953, but not before close to five hundred fifty thousand soldiers had died. All to preserve the status quo. That stalemate continues to this day.

SPUTNIK

On October 4, 1957, Russia's launching of the Sputnik into space started an undeclared war with America, for space was perceived to be the next military arena. America went into wartime mode and mobilized all its forces, civilian as well as military, in order to meet this new possible threat. On July 15, 1958, the X-15 rocketed into the stratosphere at 4,500 mph. Then on April 12, of 1961, Russia's Yuri Gagarin blasted into space. Four months later, the Berlin Wall went up. On October 14, 1962, came the Cuban Missile Crisis. For several weeks the world hunkered down. Would the two superpowers destroy each other? The crisis eventually passed, and the space race continued, with the United States winning the space lottery on July 21, 1969: Neil Armstrong and Buzz Aldrin walked on the moon.

THE VIETNAM WAR

Way back in 1954, Ike promised more support for South Vietnam. The French, after exhausting themselves there, finally gave up. America should have learned something from that defeat, but did not. By 1963 our presence had ballooned to sixteen thousand "advisors." On August 7, 1964, Congress passed the Gulf of Tonkin Resolution. In essence we declared war on North Vietnam without officially admitting that we had. Soon we had one hundred eighty thousand soldiers there; by 1968 we had sent over half a million. By then we had dumped more bombs on Vietnam than the Allies dropped during all of World War II.

While Korea had been the war no one knew was happening, with Americans preferring to ignore it, Vietnam proved to be the most unpopular war we had ever been involved in. It did much to wreck two presidencies: LBJ's and Nixon's.

Finally on April 30, 1975, Saigon fell, and on May 7, President Ford declared the war over. Thus ended the longest war in our history. During its almost eleven–year conflict, over fifty-six thousand of our military had lost their lives, and over three hundred thousand had been wounded or incapacitated. And it was during this war that a new war term came into vogue: brainwashing.

IRAQ AND AFGHANISTAN

On January 16, 1991, America's Desert Storm war began. It was incredibly fast paced, and had the full support of the United Nations. It left two hundred thousand Iraqis dead.

Since that time we liberated Afghanistan from the Taliban with comparatively few casualties. Then we returned to Iraq to get rid of Saddam Hussein. This time comparatively few of our U.N. allies joined forces with us.

As of the completion of this manuscript, our forces remain in Iraq. A new type of war is evolving: a war where insurgents, terrorists, and suicide-bombers take the place of traditional warfare.

War is always changing.

CONCLUSION

This, in brief, was our century of wars.

During this last century, over a hundred million people lost their lives in these conflagrations. Could these wars have been avoided? Most certainly. A more difficult question might be this: had we been decision-makers at the time, would our responses have been wiser than theirs? Monday morning quarterbacking generally accomplishes little.

Perhaps it would be wiser to pose the question: was there any time period where civilization and liberty were seriously at risk? A case may be made for World War I, but an even stronger one for World War II. It was there on the once blood-stained plains, cliffs, and beaches of France that two generations of allied soldiers fought and died so that freedom should not perish from the earth. And their places are marked by thousands of white crosses.

Rupert Brooke was one of that first generation to lose his life in this great cause, protecting freedom. Some of the most memorable war poems ever written bear his name. All of England mourned his death on April 23, 1915. He was only twenty-seven. Though the lines in the following poem refer to England, they could just as easily refer to America and its soldiers. I don't know of a poem about Brooke that captures the universality of battlefield loss as well as this one.

THE SOLDIER

If I should die, think only this of me;
That there's some corner of a foreign field
That is forever England. There shall be
In that rich earth a richer dust concealed;
A dust whom England bore, shaped, made aware,
Gave, once, her flowers to love, her ways to roam,
A body of England's breathing English air,
Washed by the rivers, blest by suns of home.

And think, this heart, all evil shed away,
A pulse in the eternal mind, no less
Gives somewhere back the thoughts by England given;
Her sights and sounds; dreams happy as her day;
And laughter, learnt of friends; and gentleness,
In hearts at peace, under an English heaven.

ABOUT THIS COLLECTION

This has been one of the most difficult story anthologies I've ever put together. The reason being that though untold thousands of war stories have been written, most of them have been fictional. Since we decided to feature only true stories in our collection, this dramatically narrowed our pool of stories. Furthermore, most true war stories proved to be unacceptable to us for a number of reasons; and most lacked the emotive power we were seeking.

Well, eventually we found them. A third of a century ago, I providentially acquired a small library of true-history, paperback anthologies, but I never used them until now. There they were, waiting—true stories from all the most significant wars America fought during the last century—just what I desperately needed. I never cease to be amazed by God's incredible choreography!

I think you'll agree that the mix of stories is as powerful, as memorable a collection of war stories as has yet been assembled in America.

I am interested in hearing your reactions. You may write to me at P.O. Box 1246, Conifer, CO 80433.

★
★
★

I OFFER NEITHER PAY, NOR
QUARTERS, NOR PROVISIONS;
I OFFER HUNGER, THIRST,
FORCED MARCHES, BATTLES
AND DEATH. LET HIM WHO
LOVES HIS COUNTRY [ITALY]
IN HIS HEART, AND NOT WITH
HIS LIPS ONLY, FOLLOW ME.

—GUISEPPE GARIBALDI

★

THE FLYING MADMAN

JOSEPH V. MIZRAHI

I n all the annals of wartime flight, there is no comparable story
to that of Frank Luke Jr., a young lieutenant from Phoenix,
Arizona, who approached the flimsy aircraft at the front like a
cowboy taking on a mean-spirited bucking bronco. None of those
early daredevils of the air—not even the Red Baron—excelled him in
courage. As for disregarding orders, Luke was in a class by himself.

★ ★ ★

The Madman was back!

High above the German balloon, buffeted by screaming wind
and shrapnel bursts, an American pilot rammed his Spad through a
terror-chilled sky, intent on the growing black shape beneath him.

Lit by explosions, the enemy target squatting in the night sky
resembled a sweating fat man, badly addicted to over-eating and
frozen with fear.

His airspeed indicator struggling in the red, the American pumped a rattling tracer-burst into the fleshy carcass, splitting the flabby belly. Hot gas belched out of the balloon, expanding upward in a rush of chemical stench, then exploding in violent eruptions. Easing back on the stick, the pilot watched the balloon crinkle and sag in its own funeral pyre; then, banking, he roared low over the trees toward the barest slice of light in the west.

Second Lieutenant Frank Luke, Jr. had destroyed his sixth balloon in four days that night of September 15, 1918.

Perhaps it was true that only madmen and lunatics volunteered for such missions. Certainly the sausage-shaped bags discouraged heroics. Considered important and expensive tools by the enemy, he protected them as such. Each one had its ring of antiaircraft and machine-gun batteries, all accurately ranged on the aerial approaches; in addition, a squadron of fighters stood constant alert, patrolling the area.

Possibly his German background produced Luke's craving for the bulbous giants. Whatever it was, his appetite for balloon sausage seemed insatiable. They appeared on his operational menu every night and his peculiar tastes threatened to eliminate Germany's supply in the St. Mihiel Salient.

★ ★ ★

Frank Luke came to the front in early August, 1918, a belligerent, cocky youth who still considered war a game. Based on his previous flying experience, perhaps it was. Flying new ships up to the line squadrons, and nursing the remains of wrecks back to Orly depot, was not Luke's idea of combat. True, some of the latter were so badly shot up that keeping them in the air was a decided challenge, but the possibility they might fall apart while aloft did not provide enough of the thrill he thrived on.

If the youngster from Phoenix, Arizona, had examined more closely the battered kites he flew, his mania for action might not have been so pronounced. All had flapping, shredded canvas and were pocked with bullet holes. Some retained more personal and grisly souvenirs of their encounter with the enemy. But the occasional instrument panel smeared with dried blood and bits of hair, the pilot's seat splintered by 40mm Archie (flak), and the smell of a cockpit once charred by flaming gasoline, didn't dissuade the young cowboy from requesting and getting a combat assignment.

Pilots were scarce in the First Pursuit Group just then. German circuses were formidable enemies; to prove it, men like Quentin Roosevelt and Raoul Lufbery lay buried beneath amputated propeller blades shaped into crosses the day Luke came up to take their place. He was assigned to the 27th Squadron and sent to a collection of miserable shacks bordering a bumpy pasture that served as the squadron's field.

★ ★ ★

Next day at formation, the new arrivals received their official welcome from the commander, Major Harold E. Hartney—a tough bantam, curt and waspish. "People get killed up here regularly. If you survive the first few weeks and your own personal god continues to strap himself in with you, you'll probably accomplish things. That's all, gentlemen! Good luck, you'll need it!"

Surveying the new crop of faces, Hartney's eyes narrowed on a solidly built, sharp-featured, blond youngster. As the major stared, Frank Luke grinned at him. It was a cocksure smile that told him one fledgling hadn't been impressed by the CO's grim welcome. . . .

When Hartney led their first patrol over the lines, the young skeptic was in the formation. Luke wasn't a bad kid, the major thought, but he talked too much for a newcomer; and there were men in the squadron—aces—who were getting a little tired of the Arizona gunslinger and his fast-draw mouth.

Sitting in the mess nights, and sometimes through the long,

rainy days when they were grounded, was trying enough; Luke made it worse, Hartney mused, baiting the short tempers of jittery men with what he was going to do when he met the Hun. Particularly when his confreres had already made that singular acquaintance and the braggart hadn't.

Leaving it at that, the major leveled off near Chateau-Thierry. Below him, something resembling a wobbly bicycle track reeled northward through what had once been a forest. From that altitude, the battle line seemed as commonplace as a country road.

Signaling the veterans, who boxed the youngsters, to stay up top, Major Hartney took his novices down for a closer look. Descending in gliding turns, the patrol first picked up the sound of intermittent gunfire. Next the earth's diseased, pock-marked face showed up. As they focused their unbelieving eyes, explosions erupted new sores on the festering surface. From two thousand feet, the front was an infected scab on the body of France.

Leading the flight back up to altitude, Hartney caught sight of a Spad spiraling away toward the Champagne sector. His suspicions as to the joyrider's identity were confirmed when Luke returned a half-hour later than the others. Hartney received him coldly.

"And where have you been?" he asked sarcastically.

"Sorry, Major," came the innocent reply. "I had some engine trouble. Fuel pump I think."

"Oh!" Hartney nodded his head solicitously. "All right, Luke," he snapped, "next time you stick with the formation. Dismissed."

Of course it was entirely possible that Hartney had been mistaken in his diagnosis of Luke's sudden engine trouble, but he doubted it. The second time it happened, he boiled. Eying the silent young officer before him, Hartney unlimbered. "Who do you think you are, you glory-happy little runt? When I give an order to stay in formation, I also mean you. This outfit hasn't got time or room for joystick juveniles."

The major continued to rage. When he paused to catch his breath, Luke, smiling confidently, applied the quietus.

"I got a Hun!"

"What? Where?" the major stammered.

"Near Soissons."

"Behind the German lines? How do you know you got him? Did you see him go down?"

"No," Luke said calmly, "but I sprayed him good, twice; and he was on his back, spinning down just above the trees, when I peaked for home."

Later, after reading the young aviator's report, Hartney was convinced Luke had gotten the German. Others in the squadron were not so sure. They weren't buying behind-the-line confirmations from loudmouths. More than once their jibes of "Hey, cowboy, how many red-skinned Fokkers bit the dust today?"—especially when Luke hadn't flown—burned him so much he knocked over a few tables in the mess and sent someone to the doctor.

Brooding, his pride hurt, Luke crept into a shell, avoiding the others. Although he could not speak the language, he spent most of his time with the Storks, a neighboring French escadrille, and kept to himself at home base. To this day, although officially confirmed, some discount his first victory. There are no doubters concerning the others.

The unruly cub might have become a lone wolf had he not met someone equally embittered. Lieutenant Joe Wehner's luck turned sour the day he acknowledged himself as the young man Uncle Sam was pointing to. Wehner is a German name, but there were a host of them in the AEF: Luke and Rickenbacker, among others. Unfortunately for Joe, his name had intrigued some highly unintelligent intelligence officer, whose powers of deduction were nil.

By some twisted logic, the sleuth concluded that Wehner was a spy. All of Joe's movements were suspicious. Therefore he was followed, his baggage searched, his mail read, and when nothing was found, they arrested him. He was under arrest when his unit left Texas. Joining it in New York, he was again apprehended. Finally permitted to sail, he was detained, questioned, and searched upon his arrival in France, then released with the warning that his movements would be closely watched.

Sitting in the mess, Wehner doubted the man across from him and lay awake nights questioning the snores from the next cot. He was jumpy and suspicious. The endless badgering had made a recluse of him. Aloof, shut up in his world of misgiving and persecution, it was natural that he should seek out the squadron's other outcast. Both had grown grim and taciturn: one through the jeering disbelief of his comrades; the other through fear and suspicion. Together in the air, they were to take out their frustrations on the enemy.

When the American drive in the St. Mihiel Salient opened, Major Hartney moved up to group and the 27th squadron got a new CO, Captain Alfred Grant. Grant was a rule-book soldier, a good one. He followed regulations and expected the same obedience from his subordinates. Therefore, it was inevitable that he and Luke should clash.

On September 11, 1918, the 27th moved into the Verdun sector near Rembercourt. Luke had been out joyriding that day and had missed Grant's briefing for coming operations in the sector. As usual, during a routine patrol, he had quit formation and made his own tour of the countryside, ending up by visiting the Storks and returning to field late at night.

Grant was waiting for him. In the cramped Nissen hut that served as his office, he told Luke what to expect if his escapades continued:

"I don't know what Hartney let you get away with, Luke, but I'm not giving you the time of day. Any more of this solo action and you can kiss those gold bars good-by. If that's clear, get the blazes out of here!"

Luke's temper flared for a moment; then, saluting quickly, he turned and walked stiffly toward the mess. In the reconverted hangar, crowded with smoke and old furniture, something resembling *Dardanella* was being tortured on the ancient piano and an enthusiastic but raucous quartet of pilots seemed to howl approval by their accompaniment. Joe Wehner wasn't around, so Luke ordered cognac and sat by himself, brooding.

Grant with his piddling regulations—he'd like to get the smug leader in the air. He'd fly circles around the rule book. Where did that idiot think he went when he left those time-wasting formations? You'd never see Grant's plane twenty miles behind the German lines. Luke earned his flight pay, and the only reason he visited the Storks so much was to gas up, so he could stay in the air longer. Besides, he enjoyed their company; the French weren't like the captain's rule-book robots.

What's more, he was better than anyone in this lousy squadron—aces, the whole darn bunch, including Rickenbacker. All he needed was a chance to prove it.

While Luke nursed his cognac and soothed his ego, the conversation at a nearby table drifted into his thoughts. Captain Jerry Vasconcelles refilled his glass and repeated the statement that had drawn Luke from his troubles. "I don't care what you say, Triplane, Albatross, new D VII, they're still aircraft; they've got limitations, and you know what to expect attacking them. But a balloon. Have you ever seen the stuff that hits those bags?" Vasconcelles bent his fingers as he counted, "Archie, machine guns, flaming onions; then there's a fighter circus to contend with, and you never face a bum one. No, balloons are too dangerous! You can get them, but they usually get you. A couple of tracers, hot gas and woosh—you go up with it. They're the toughest all right. The man who gets one has my respect."

The listeners solemnly agreed, and as it usually did, the talk turned to women. As Luke walked toward his quarters, Vasconcelles's words echoed in his head. "They're the toughest. The man who gets one has my respect." Luke nodded and the war's most amazing string of victories began.

"Temperature, oil pressure, magneto all okay." As Luke checked his instruments, his mechanic climbed along the wing and thrust his head into the cockpit, out of the wind. "Where to today?"

"We're having sausage for dinner. I'm getting us a balloon!"

Luke revved the engine and his mechanic dropped from the fuselage amid the smoke shaken from the twin exhausts, the wind plastering his coveralls to him. He pulled the chocks, and maneuvering with abrupt, swinging turns, Luke taxied the ship to the edge of the field and pointed her into the wind. The engine blipped in doubtful idle, then roared, its propwash pressing the grass flat. The Spad vibrated numbly; then quivering and shaking, it began to roll forward, bumping along the field, steadily increasing speed until it was airborne, plumes of black smoke dissipating gently behind it.

The afternoon dwindled away over the dark wooded clumps of the Argonne, with Luke sighting an occasional speck in the distance. But nothing materialized. He had paralleled the lines for fifty miles and was turning back in disgust when he saw it. Moored to a skeleton village, a soft, gray shape bobbed on its cables, riding at anchor in the light breeze. A series of climbing turns transformed the bag into a plump oval.

Luke pushed the stick to the firewall, stood the Spad on its nose and dove at full throttle. Wind screamed through the bracing wire. The ship buckled and the balloon spiraled up like a punted football. Bursting shrapnel littered the sky, dirty black fog smudging the patchwork of expanding ground. Percussion thumped the air. Beneath the swollen hulk a frantic observer tried to jump from the wicker basket and fouled in the rigging.

Luke sucked the joy stick into his belly, hung on his prop and raked the onrushing bulge. A loop and a half-roll aligned the sagging balloon so he could make another pass. His second burst slashed the wounded side before his temperamental guns jammed. While the Heinie winch crews struggled to lower the collapsing monster, Luke climbed in a chandelle and rapped the gun stoppage free with a mallet. Then he roared down on his back, his tracers pokering the ruptured bag as it fell to the ground. There was a white-hot, upward slam, a fiery gas cloud; the balloon incinerated and vanished in tumbling sparks.

Before returning to his field, Luke armed himself with two confirmations from a nearby American balloon squadron that had witnessed the action. The Spad's engine having been hit, he rode a side-car in. His squadron, learning of his spectacular victory by phone, jammed headquarters when he reported. Amid the back-slapping, hair-mussing, hand-shaking congratulations, Luke forgot his personal grudges and dropped his defiant attitude. He'd scored a tremendous victory and his companions were proud of him.

The Spad came home the following day, after some emergency repairs enabled it to make the field. Luke's mechanics, who had crowed over their machine's victory, were dumbstruck at its appearance. More canvas was gone than remained. The top left wing consisted of air, wire and three stringers. The empennage was a sieve and a huge gash had been ripped through the pilot's seat, less than six inches from Luke's body.

Shaking his head, Luke's ground chief inspected the damage with serious misgivings. "Lieutenant, I've seen a lot of birds come in, but when they're like this, the pilot who flies 'em doesn't climb out of the cockpit."

Grinning, Luke poked his fingers through the splintered seat. "You take care of the aircraft, chief. I'll take care of me. If I were going to get killed, this would have been it."

One balloon, however, was only an appetizer. Luke relished German sausage, and when the opportunity to glut himself appeared, he was prepared. An enemy bag was holding up the Allied drive near Buzy. From its strategic vantage point, it could observe all infantry deployment and relay the information to German artillery. Performing its duties to perfection, it had kept the Allies from bringing up reinforcements and supplies.

Circling the location of the balloon on his operations map, Captain Grant drew an X over it. "That's what I want, Luke. Mark it off. Get that bag and get it tonight. You can take one man with you."

"Joe Wehner?"

"All right."

The sun was half down over Buzy. Leaving Wehner as top cover, Luke fell over on his back and went in. One burst and the balloon began to crumple. Burning in its own stink, it collapsed in a torn flutter. Only this time, the Germans had seen Luke. A swarm of Fokkers dived on the lone Spad, their stingers (bullets) burning through his tail. The instrument panel splintered away, and as Luke rolled for position, his guns jammed again. Defenseless, he plunged for the trees. Steady chattering fire shattered the air behind him. Turning, he saw a plane breaking into the enemy formation and one of the black-crossed Fokkers spinning aimlessly, trailing smoke.

High above, Joe Wehner had slipped into the Hun flight. Flying tight, he had managed the masquerade long enough to get their leader. In the confusion and darkness, the two Americans shook off pursuit and rendezvoused over Abancourt, where Luke spotted a second balloon. It died hard. Finally, on the sixth pass, it collapsed—leaking fire from a dozen rents. With the few bursts left in his guns, Luke shot up the ground battery which had given him the most trouble; then they turned for home. Score for the day: two balloons and a fighter.

The kids were good and Grant had another assignment for them. They were ordered to bring down a bag just raised over Boigneville. Instead of making the dual attack as directed, Wehner and Luke separated. North of Verdun, Wehner punctured his first bag and turned for the second he and Luke had chosen as ripe for popping. As he approached, a red flame mushroomed over the position; Luke had beaten him to it.

Banking sharply, throttle wide open, Wehner raced for the location of the third balloon the pair had mapped for destruction. The steady pump of antiaircraft shells told him that Luke had already called. Smoke and flames obscured the approach. Then far below, nose down for speed, a ship with bull's-eye marking burst from the billowing clouds, pursued by a pack of Albatross and Fokker triplanes.

Zooming in toward them from above, Wehner did an Immelman and got behind. His tracers cut a triplane in two and a short burst killed the pilot of an Albatross. The bat-winged craft tipped on its side, then half-rolled into a steep dive. Their engines hammering, Wehner and Luke fled toward the American line, where friendly antiaircraft discouraged further pursuit.

Score for the day: Wehner two fighters and a balloon; Luke two balloons. But Luke wasn't finished. He gassed up, reloaded and, precisely at 7:50, his sixth balloon in four days plummeted from the sky in flames.

More astonishing, Luke and Wehner had a combined one-night score of four balloons and two fighters!

Once it had been considered impossible. Balloons just didn't go down that easily. Luke's last one had withstood repeated attacks by French, English, Belgian and American fliers for months. Then along came this green kid and his friend, and three more go down with it.

They shook their heads while toasting Frank Luke and Joe Wehner that night. It was uncanny. On the other side of the line, they just shook their heads and drank. Now, whenever two Spads were seen on patrol, the German balloon line was hastily lowered.

But Luke and Wehner were already hatching plans to counteract this. They went straight to the Group Commander with their idea. Major Hartney, their old Squadron CO, listened to the proposal—so audacious and inconceivable that he shivered. The kid to whom he had explained the dangers of flying combat was now outlining a suicide pact for Wehner and himself. He proposed to attack three German balloons at dusk and return to base, flying blind in the dark!

"I know we can do it, Major. I got my last balloon in the dark and made it back."

"You almost cracked up, too," Hartney reminded him. "How will you see the field, let alone get near it?"

"Just fire flares and rockets. We've figured it out. Joe will get the first balloon about 7:10. I'll get the second say 7:20, and between us the third should go at half-past. You'll be able to see the fires. And when the last one goes up, light the field."

Hartney rubbed his chin, dazed. What was there to say? This twenty-one-year-old cowboy had just mapped out a campaign with the calm aplomb of a Caesar. One that by all the rule books had no chance of succeeding. But what startled Hartney most was that he believed in it and would give his consent.

Take-off was slated for 6:45. Two leather teddy bears bundled across the field, sank into their cockpits and perked their thumbs. The chocks bounced free. Tail up, the two ships jockeyed across the meadow, past a silent huddle of pilots, and disappeared over the trees. Once the drone of their motors receded, the huddle shuffled and dispersed, moving aimlessly in vague circles. Slowly the minutes ticked by. Watch dials were turned up, scrutinized, then plunged back into heavy overcoats until they should be ready.

Time ticked by with agonizing slowness . . . 7:00 . . . 7:05 . . . 7:10 . . .

"Look, they've got one!" North of Verdun, a torch licked the purpling dusk. At 7:21, flame disturbed the sky once more. By 7:30, the field bristled with anticipation. Five minutes passed but still no beacon flared to symbolize the clean sweep. Hartney glanced at the rockets lining the field ready for launching. A circle of ciga-rette ends glowed, brightened, then waned, revealing the unsteady breathing of their smokers.

Seven thirty-six, a stab of pulsating flame. Hartney rushed toward the rocket launchers, but they had already seen it. As the red bulb flickered and grew, a July 4th celebration erupted over the squadron's field. Rockets steamed into the night, exploding, crack-ling, bursting, scribbling their receipt of Luke's message and wink-ing their congratulations.

Hartney bellowed like a madman. "Burn it all, headquarters, the mess, the billets, the hangars, everything, but light this field up."

Cognac flowed, cowboy yelps punctured the genteel French air. Men danced, kissing one another. As Colonel Billy Mitchell's Cadillac pulled into the 27th's area, pandemonium, just unhar-nessed, gamboled like a colt.

Almost forgetting his salute, Hartney pointed to the descending fire. "Did you see it, Colonel? Done, just as they said it would. They're phenomenal." Indeed they were. A few minutes later Mitchell congratulated the two warriors, who were quickly transformed into embarrassed second lieutenants as they told their story.

The first balloon had gone down easily under both their guns. Luke had gotten the second and Wehner the third. American anti-aircraft almost bagged them on the way back, scoring several hits on both planes; otherwise the mission had gone as planned.

Corps headquarters was duly impressed by what they termed "a unique air maneuver by pilots under its command." In the trenches, acknowledgment was of a more earthy variety. Every time the doughboys saw two Spads headed for the German lines at sundown, they knew it was the flying madman. Lying in the mud, the foot sol-diers looked up at the balloon busters and shouted, "There goes Luke and Wehner. Give 'em hell, baby. Ride 'em cowboy." And while they lived, they did.

The afternoon of September 18, 1918, was Luke's greatest in the air. In less than ten minutes, he destroyed two balloons and three aircraft. Yet he suffered his most bitter defeat. Five of the enemy went down that day, but so did a friend.

Wehner and Luke were out balloon hunting earlier than usual, when they sighted two peacefully bobbing, one above the other, near Labeuville. Luke's first burst crumpled the top bag and the second was rapidly hauled down as he looped and followed it in.

Ninety feet above the ground, it too exploded. Spiraling upward through the flaming gas, Luke climbed for altitude, looking for his partner. He had expected Joe to take the second balloon. Why hadn't he? Then, high above, he saw Wehner. Wheeling in behind him was a flock of checkerboard Fokkers. They had him trapped. The formation split and a pair came down on Luke.

Flame spattered from the lead ship's guns, ripping into the Spad's upper wing. Eyes focused on the German's yellow spinner, Luke squeezed off a double burst. The planes roared in at each other, closing head on.

The German ate Luke's bullets and spit steel-jacketed slugs back at him. Luke felt his ship stagger and hesitate. His opponent's angry, yellow cowl was on top of him, machine guns hammering, vibrating with rage. He drove straight for it, choking on the vile phosphorous from his own overheated guns. Suddenly the Fokker jolted to a mid-air stop, swerved violently to the left, and plummeted to the ground, unwinding in a slow, smoking spiral. Luke had escaped a collision by less than twenty yards.

There was no time for congratulations, however. Howling by from above, the second Fokker's guns chewed up his rudder. Banking sharply, Luke fired a short, accurate burst. The German tipped up on one unsteady wing, hung there, then streaming hot oil and flame, raced to destruction below.

Again Luke climbed for altitude. The dogfight had taken him

too low. Far above, the remainder of the Hun formation milled about idly. Wehner was gone. He had probably slipped away when the Germans spotted him, Luke thought. Well, he'd also had enough for one day; it was time to go home.

Over the Allied lines he ran into heavy antiaircraft fire. It meant only one thing—enemy raider. Sure enough, away to the east, a German observation plane had turned and was heading for the safety of its own lines. Luke had position on the Halberstadt. His first burst spilled the observer before he could swing his guns around. His second stapled the pilot. It was a classic demonstration of the textbook method for attacking two-seaters.

Then the Spad started to buck, the engine spitting. The main tank had been hit. Luke switched to his ten-minute reserve and nursed her down on an abandoned auxiliary field near Verdun.

His ship's appearance was typical after an evening out, and he rolled back to the 27th in a side car. The field was quiet. Groups of pilots passed him, nodded, and hurried on. At the headquarters shack they took his verbal report without elaboration. There was no joking, none of the usual questions. It was cold business. The attitude puzzled Luke. He'd just had his greatest day and people acted as though they had come from a funeral.

After a cursory debriefing, Hartney motioned him into his office. "There's a few things we'll have to talk over, Frank." It was difficult for Hartney to begin, and while he weighed his opening sentence, Luke removed the unpleasant burden from him.

"Do you mind if I finish my combat reports first, sir? I want to check those confirmations with Lieutenant Wehner!"

Hartney nodded and let him go. Someone else would have to tell him.

Joe's room was empty. There were pilots in the billets who knew about Wehner, but none said anything. It was at the hangars that Luke heard the news from Wehner's mechanic. Joe had gone down burning over Labeuville. Yes, it was Frank Luke's greatest day in the air: two balloons, three planes, and a friend.

In his twenty-one years, Frank Luke had known setbacks but never defeat. Now all his triumphs were hollow. The enemy had erased them with one blow, and he had been powerless to stop it. Of what use had his string of incredible victories been, his skill and daring in the air? They hadn't bought immunity for his friend. Joe Wehner had died like countless others, burning in flaming gas, and all of Luke's confirmations had not been able to prevent it.

Combat's achievements were balanced on a day-to-day basis. Today's success could not be entered in tomorrow's ledger and yesterday's fame, however great, did not awe the future. More so than if it had been himself, Wehner's dying rid Luke of the idea that war was a game, where only the other fellow got hurt. It became instead a personal vendetta between Luke and the Germans, a private blood feud that forced him to seek more overwhelming odds and greater challenges as penance for his friend's death.

For three days, though, Luke sat alone in his room, staring, muttering, questioning. Hartney ordered him to Paris on leave, but gaiety's capital held no joys for the disillusioned warrior. With perhaps fifty American pilots AWOL in Paris and the rest scheming to join them, Luke returned before half his leave had expired. His explanation, "There wasn't anything to do."

But there was plenty to be done at the front. Luke had big plans.

"Remember that old auxiliary drome I used near Verdun?"

Hartney nodded.

"If you put a flight in there, we can dominate the whole German balloon front. We'll be looking right down their throats. As soon as they send one up, we can pop it. The field is ten miles closer to the lines, and we can jump their observation planes and bombers as soon as they're spotted."

The major shook his head. "You're right about the position,

Frank. It makes an excellent base. Only the krauts know it too. They've smashed it flat a dozen times."

"But it hasn't been used in months. The hangars are still standing and a few planes could run wild before they were shelled out. If you don't want to send a flight, let me go alone."

Once before Luke had outlined a crazy plan to Hartney and three balloons had burned as predicted. Results were what counted, and Luke got them. How was his business. Seeing that Group stayed atop the victory column was the major's.

"All right, Luke," he said. "You'll go up with Vasconcelles's flight."

When he left, Luke thought about flying under Vasconcelles. The captain's admiration for pilots who voluntarily attacked balloons had launched his career. Perhaps it was a good omen.

Lieutenant Ivan Roberts became Luke's new running mate in his twilight balloon strikes. On their first patrol together, the pair attacked a flight of Fokkers. Luke got one, but Roberts was never seen again.

Secluding himself in his quarters, remembering how Joe Wehner had gone down in another dogfight, Luke saw it all clearly. He was jinxed. Victory for him was automatic death for his partners. From now on he would fly alone.

On September 28th, he disappeared on an unauthorized flight, returning the following day with a confirmed kill. He'd burned a partially inflated balloon in its nest near Bantheville, swooping within fifty feet of the ground to destroy it.

Rather pleased with himself, Luke tossed his combat report on Captain Grant's desk. Only this time the squadron CO had taken enough. Luke might be the finest pilot who ever sat in a cockpit, but Grant was fed up with him.

"Where have you been?" he barked angrily.

"There's a war on, Captain." Luke's tone was arrogant. "I've been out doing my bit."

Grant exploded. "Listen to me, hot shot. Don't swagger in here and brag to me. Maybe you're the greatest thing flying since wings. In the air you may be better than the birds, but you're the lousiest officer I've ever seen. Down here you stink! And until you learn to act like a man instead of a spoiled child, you don't fly. You're grounded!"

Trembling with rage, Grant returned Luke's tight salute and watched his stiff back as he marched out the door.

Furious at the reprimand, but controlling his temper, Luke hurried to his plane. Disregarding a mechanic's warning that the Spad needed gas and oil, he climbed into the cockpit and ran a quick pre-flight. He'd fill up at Verdun. The motor roared and he bounced across the field, steadily pulling the nose up. At fifty feet, he banked and headed for Vasconcelles's flight at the auxiliary drome.

No sooner was Luke airborne, than Grant was on the phone to Vasconcelles. "Hello, Jerry—I've grounded Luke. He's on his way up to the field now. I want him arrested when he gets there. That's right! I'll send someone up to fly his ship back." Grant hung up and turned to his adjutant. "What else can I do? That kid's got to learn that this isn't a private war."

"What happens now?" the adjutant asked doubtfully.

"I'm recommending him for the Distinguished Service Cross, and then I'm going to see that he's court-martialed."

When Luke arrived at the field, Vasconcelles was waiting with the news. "You're under arrest, Frank. I'm sorry—it's straight from Grant. You're going back in a side car; that's all I know."

Luke's questions were interrupted by the sound of Major Hartney's Camel as he settled the little ship down on the shell-ploughed field. Hartney was checking on the flight's operational setup and knew nothing of Grant's action. Vasconcelles didn't tell him. The matter was between Grant and Luke, and he wanted no part of it.

As soon as he realized the flight commander would make no mention of his arrest, Luke seized the opportunity to present Hartney with a plan he had been working on.

"There're three *Drachens* near Verdun, major. I've been watching their movements for the past couple of days and think I can get them if you let me go now!"

Listening to the youngster's voice, Hartney thought he detected a note of urgency. But it seemed Luke was always in a hurry to go somewhere. The lad was amazing. He didn't belong in the army; he was his own little self-contained destruction force. From the moment he came up, the kid knew it all. Hartney remembered that confident grin at the first briefing, the first joyride, and the first reprimand. There had been many of the latter in the short time Luke had been at the front. Less than two months—and already an ace three times over.

It was incredible. Hartney spent his time pouring over reports, analyzing, considering. A crew of experts worked for him. Intelligence and staff all had ideas and when they jelled into an operational plan, it was given to him to disseminate among his squadron commanders, flight leaders, and individual pilots. But the chain of command never seemed to reach Luke. He had his own operations worked out on the side. They were never coordinated, mapped or tested; they were not all-encompassing in scope. They did not require prodigious preparation. All they needed was Frank Luke in his Spad.

Hartney might brief the others, but Luke briefed the major. His attack plans were as spontaneous and unrehearsed as a sandlot footballer's strategy.

"Run over the goal and I'll hit you with a long one. There are three *Drachens* near Verdun. I think I can get them all."

Plans—simple, casual, unmilitary, but Luke had never failed to score with them. Hartney smiled to himself. In reality, war was a disorganized, impersonal, unpredictable mess with little place for rulebook soldiers. Enjoying a vicious free-for-all ten thousand feet above the earth, was halfway to coming out of it alive. Luke enjoyed it. That made him different from the rest.

The major nodded. "You can go, Frank, but wait till the sun drops. It's still too early."

At 5:22 Luke was in the air. Ten minutes later a note, dropped over American Balloon Headquarters from a low-flying Spad, sent the observers diving for cover. Picking themselves up from the dirt, the startled group read the following: "Watch three Hun balloons on the Meuse. Luke."

The first balloon was at Dun. With Luke's initial burst it unraveled in plunging flame. He rolled and headed for the second near Briere Farm, climbing his Spad deep into the darkening sky. Far below, the fire blossoming from his first victim began to fade, the flames dropping to earth. It was the signal for every gun in the German balloon line to open.

Except for a thin slice of moon, the sky at fifteen thousand feet was cold and black. Shielded by the night, Luke dropped his nose and plunged like some sinister bird into the devil's cauldron below. It bubbled, hissed, and spat. Gouts of molten steel roared up at him, splashing the night with fire. But the flames concerning Luke most were from his own ship. Twin jets of blue flared fitfully from his exhaust stacks. The Spad's engine had been hit and was missing. As his ring sight filled with the balloon's looming hulk, the plane shuddered. Something crunched into his ribs. He fell forward; the ship stalled and began spinning.

Archie was silent now and the squadron of German fighters which had pounced on him from above watched as the American ace, his dead hand on the stick, cartwheeled toward the ground. Only Luke wasn't dead. Tumbling past the balloon, he kicked opposite rudder, popped the stick forward and swooped up like a bat under the great belly. His tracer ammunition burned it open and guts of flame spilled out over the winch crews below.

Luke was already banking for number three balloon at Milly before the German batteries could resume firing. He followed his probing tracers right up to his gigantic target before veering off sharply.

WHOOM—the explosion kicked him upward, scorching his unprotected face. The Spad dangled drunkenly in the air, faltered and lurched toward the ground. Fighting the controls, Luke righted her just above the trees. He slumped in his seat and fumbled with the heavy sheepskin collar of his flying suit, letting the ship fly herself. She was a naked skeleton, trailing struts and bracing wire. Blood and oil covered the instrument panel and Luke felt sticky and wet inside his jacket.

It was impossible to gain altitude. It would be useless anyway he thought. If he ran into some Germans, he'd just have that much further to fall. One sharp turn, one roll and the wings would come off. No, he would have to limp home over the trees—no trucks, no excursions, nothing fancy, straight-line, simple flying. That was fine with him; he'd had enough excitement for one night. Besides, there was a better chance down low where he was. He'd be difficult to spot. If the Spad held together and the motor kept running, he'd be all right.

Wiping the blood from the instrument panel, Luke checked his gauges. He had enough oil pressure, but the engine temperature was high. Nevertheless he would soon be over the American line.

Ahead of him, packed with Germany infantry, was a road that became the principle street of a village. He was lined up directly with it. Wouldn't have to turn much. The Spad had enough altitude and there were still a few bursts left in his guns. All he need do was nose down a little. One pass, that was all.

Gently, Luke opened his throttle and eased forward on the stick. His machine guns chattered, scattering the dark knot of men below and leaving a dozen infantrymen sprawled on the shadowy cobblestones. But that little extra speed to enable him to regain the altitude his ship lost in its shallow dive proved too much for the battered Spad. The left wing wobbled badly, threatening to shear off completely.

Beyond the town a large, undulating meadow spread out toward the banks of the Meuse. Luke glided into it, bouncing over the uneven ground. He shut the engine down; then, gripping his service pistol, he slid from the cockpit. Pain seared his ribs; he could hardly breathe. He shook his head to keep from blacking out and stumbled toward a narrow brook that fed the river. Cold water would clear his brain, sharpen his senses and make him think.

As he trudged over the damp grass, indistinct shouts sounded over the meadow behind him. Luke turned and fired a clip at a group of loping figures. Spurts of flame pricked the darkness. There was a final spattering of bullets and then nothing. . . .

They carried him missing for three months, but Frank Luke was dead. All through the night of September 19, 1918, rockets and flares blazed up from his home field at Rembercourt, spouting their question marks into the darkness. His confirmations came in, but Luke never acknowledged his field's frantic beckoning and the heavens remained silent. Armistice came and still no news. Then, in January, 1919, a Graves Registration officer discovered the body of an unknown American aviator killed near Murvaux on September 19.

Villagers testified that, prior to his death, the pilot had brought down the three balloons, strafed a German infantry column in the town square, and, upon landing, had fought with his pistol until killed. Their description of the pilot fitted Luke, and a letter and watch found with the body subsequently identified him. But the record was not yet officially closed.

From those who had opposed his conduct most—Hartney and Grant—came a Congressional Medal of Honor recommendation. It was awarded, the only such honor ever won while under military arrest, and the only one made to a World War I aviator. With it went the Distinguished Service Cross.

No one deserved them more. In a space of less than three weeks, one of which he did not fly, Luke had destroyed fourteen balloons and five planes. More imposing victory lists have been run up, but for sheer derring-do, nothing has equaled that record.

Frank Luke was a born warrior. The relentless hunger which urged him to the brink of destruction in combat so compelled him that he was eventually forced even beyond the terrible demands of a soldier. There, far above the call of duty, he found his element.

★ ★ ★

Joseph V. Mizrahi wrote during the middle years of the twentieth century.

★
★
★

THE ART OF WAR IS SIMPLE
ENOUGH. FIND OUT WHERE
YOUR ENEMY IS. GET AT HIM
AS SOON AS YOU CAN. STRIKE
AT HIM AS HARD AS YOU CAN
AND AS OFTEN AS YOU CAN,
AND KEEP MOVING ON . . .

—ULYSSES S. GRANT

THE YANKS
GO THROUGH

WILLIAM SLAVENS McNUTT

For four long bloody years, men had fought each other for every inch of French ground, were often driven back, and had to fight again and again for the same patch of blood-red soil. The tide finally turned in 1917 when America entered what contemporaries called "The Great War," and in posterity "World War I."

It was a year later before the Allied armies finally began to make progress. One of the most incredible word pictures of war ever penned is this one by war correspondent William McNutt for *Collier's*.

★ ★ ★

I have seen the game of war played in the open fields under a clear sky as a writer or painter might order it for his own purpose; seen it played in a sunlit gold and green valley of France by men of my own land as a moving-picture director might have arranged it for the eye of his camera. I have sat on an open hillside under a screaming roof of loaded steel and watched our farthest thin brown line of fighting infantry smash irresistibly into the worst the Germans had to offer; flank and rush frantically chattering machine guns, dodge far-flung blows of barrage fire as a boxer dodges a fist: dodge and rush and strike—and win!

I have seen all that as one might sit in the bleachers and watch a football game played out on the field below; seen it as the occupant of a choice seat in a huge, natural amphitheater, watching what will be important history carved out in action before my eyes.

It was during the German retreat from the Marne, out of the Soissons-Rheims salient, and it had been in progress for a number of days. The Germans were getting back as best they might, leaving behind them quantities of munitions and equipment, fighting chiefly rear-guard actions with machine guns. And always at their heels, twenty-four hours of each victorious day, were the French and Americans, slugging them back with whining tons of high explosive, showering them with the death that the buzzing shrapnel bears, stinging them to greater speed by the high-whistling little metal words with which a machine gun argues, stabbing and smashing them out of town and wood with bayonet and gun butt.

So swift was the advance that as dignified and complex an institution as a division headquarters might move several times in one day, and the front line was as hard to locate as an address in Brooklyn! And behind that ever-moving thin brown line of fighting infantry to a depth of thirty miles there was spread out a magnitude of movement that stunned the imagination; a bewildering military panorama that attacked the eye with vast picture after vast picture until at last one watched unseeing, wrung dry of the capacity for further impression.

I first came upon this grumbling sea of mighty movement while riding toward the front in a correspondent's car. It was near Belleau

Wood, the scene of the first signal American success on the Marne. The machine sped up to the crest of a hill, and there, just ahead of us, blotting out the white of the French road with a moving stain of brown, was a long column of American artillery stretching ahead as far as the eye could reach. Shortly we overtook and rode beside it. They had been on the way for days. Grimy, dust-powdered men were sprawled out fast asleep on the jolting caissons. Weary officers were nodding in their saddles as they rode. The heads of the horses were all adroop as they plodded on. The soldiers afoot were walking bent forward, slowly, wearily, mechanically slogging on through the dust like automatons driven by a mechanism that had almost run down but would never, never quite stop and so moved them irresistibly onward, slow, thumping step after slow, thumping step, wearily on and on over the flinty road through the choking, gritty haze of dust.

For the space of half an hour we whirled by this monotonous, slow-moving but ever forward-slogging line of weary, dust-smothered life, and groaning, creaking mechanism of wheel and spring, of gun and wagon body.

Beyond the column of artillery we passed a long line of machine gunners, men riding humped up on funny little dwarf one-horse carts no bigger than a baby carriage (they reminded me at first of circus clowns in a parade and then of burlesque charioteers); beyond the machine gunners, motor lorries, huge brown vehicles, swaying, groaning, growling sullenly along on their way to the distant front, some packed with weary, lolling soldiers, some piled high with supplies. Then big guns jouncing slowly along in tow of clanking, grinding tractors. Then more troops and artillery and more and more. Seemingly there was no end to this slow-moving, brown line of energy crawling up toward the battlefield. And it was all American. In one day I rode probably seventy-five miles, every yard of the way past this grumbling, dust-befogged procession. For other days I rode through this staggering immensity of action, going from correspondents' headquarters to the front and back again. And then my hour of luck arrived!

The Germans were making a desperate stand on the Ourcq on the line running to the right from Fère-en-Tardenois. I arrived near noon in the shell-wrecked town where was located the headquarters of the American division that was then thunderously, savagely slugging the *Boche* [Germans] with its every power of man and gun to stun him loose from his desperate grip on the far slope of the Ourcq. Together with two friends I visited the division intelligence officer and for the twentieth time inquired as to a point of vantage from which we might really see some of the infantry action. The town was semi-circled with American heavy artillery, and it was necessary to talk in quick bursts of speech between the obliterating attacks of sound that roared forth at rapid intervals from the hot mouths of the fighting metal monsters.

"Our infantry's going over this afternoon about here," he said, indicating on the map a spot on the far side of the Ourcq to the right of Fère-en-Tardenois. "If you could get up to the Château-Forêt, you might see a little of the work."

"How about Hill 212?" I asked. I had heard about that hill from an officer friend, and I wanted to get there. The intelligence officer smiled and shook his head.

"Not a chance. Great observation if you could get there—which you couldn't—and if you did the betting's all against your getting back. Better try Château-Forêt. The view's not as good from there, but you'll probably live longer to tell about what little you do see."

Speaking in the short intervals between gunfire, he gave us our directions, and our car crawled slowly through a village to the fork in the road at the foot of a hill; then we took the road up the hill to the right. I had thought there was a certain degree of noise in the valley below where the heavy guns were located and where quivering nerves were beaten to numbness. I was mistaken! Until I reached the plateau at the top of that hill I had no conception of noise. For that plateau, stretching out before us for some two thousand yards to a wood ahead, was sown thick, with rapid-firing seventy-fives. From copse and gun pit and open field all about us they were spitting flame and steel.

And it was a different world up there on that flame-spouting plateau. The traffic was less, and it moved faster. The men were more alert. The plateau was clean! We had come through thirty miles of a world that was dirty, dust-caked, greasy, slow-moving; a world that was stupid with monotony and fatigue, a sluggish, low grumbling world of hard, mean service. And on this plateau was the beginning of the clean, swift, deadly world of action for which that hard, slow-grinding service was rendered. There was a soul tonic in the spiritual atmosphere of that clean world.

We whirled across the plateau and into the wood beyond. None of the soldiers we met knew anything about Château-Forêt, so we kept on going. We arrived at last at a crossroad where a sweating M. P. halted us. "Château-Forêt?" he bawled in my ear. "Don't know nothin' about it. Mebbe find out down at brigade headquarters. Take this road to the left through the woods an' leave your car at the first-aid dressin' station. They'll tell you how to reach brigade."

Three hundred yards down the road to the left and we reached the first-aid dressing station, a mere hut in the woods. The newly wounded were there, lying on stretchers on the ground awaiting transportation to the rear. And immediately about that rude dressing station, in the midst of all that cannon fire, among those newly wounded there was a curious illusion of peace. On the faces of all the wounded there was a common expression of ecstatic tranquility, of exalted content. They had done the ultimate thing well; for them at that moment nothing mattered; and from them radiated an aura of peace, so that one had the feeling of being remote from the war; of being safe in a spiritual shelter.

"Brigade headquarters is right ahead along that path through the woods there," an orderly directed us. "Château-Forêt? Never heard of it."

We went on along the little path through the thick wood, a path walled by a dense growth of underbrush, past quantities of German ammunition and equipment, past infantrymen curled up in the scanty shelter of individual pits, past men sleeping sprawled out in the underbrush, men in whom fatigue had conquered caution. We came then upon a lieutenant who discouraged us.

"Château-Forêt?" he exclaimed. "Why, that's away over to your left, and you couldn't get into the observation post there anyway. The general's up there now and a lot of others. It's full up. No, I don't know of a place from where you could see the infantry go over. You can go on up to the edge of the woods, but you couldn't see much of anything from there. I'd advise you to go back."

"Well, we'll go up to the edge of the woods anyway."

"You can do that. I'll tell you what: I'll take you up to the brigade, and we'll see what they can do for you."

A hundred yards farther along the path we stopped. There was a narrow trench there perhaps ten feet long and partly roofed with sheet iron.

"This," said the lieutenant, pointing at the partly roofed trench at our feet, "is brigade headquarters. Wait for me a minute."

He squirmed in at one end of the trench, and almost immediately a major popped out at the other.

"Hello!" said the major. "Do you know Floyd Gibbons? Where is he now?"

I told him. He asked after other correspondents I knew. A colonel crawled up out of the trench and joined us, and for five minutes we left the battle flat on its back and stood there gossiping eagerly about mutual acquaintances. (I know of nothing more strange than the usual conversations in which one indulges at the front in the heat of battle. Recently I was racing down a road to get out from under heavy shell fire, falling on my face every five or ten yards as a whistling scream announced a fresh arrival. A panting lieutenant caught step with me. "Do you know So-and-So?" he gasped. "Yes," I replied as a shell whirred down out of the sky and we both fell flat on our faces. "Where is he now?" he continued as the sound of the explosion died away and we rose, running together. "I think he's in Paris," I answered, and even as I spoke rolled flat with him in a muddy ditch as another shell screamed down and broke near by. And thus we continued our way for several hundred yards, discussing our friend and his characteristics between dives into the mud.) After a little our lieutenant guide appeared, followed by Captain X., an artillery officer. Captain X. was heavy of chest and slightly bowed as to underpinning. "I can take you where you can see something," he assured us. "I won't guarantee to bring you back. It's not healthy out where I'm going, but the view's fine. All right? Come ahead." We said good-by to the major and the colonel and trailed on after the captain through the woods. After a walk of perhaps a hundred and fifty yards we came to the edge of the forest and stepped suddenly out into the open field. There was no gradual thinning of the trees to warn us that we were about to reach the clear. The edge of that forest was as definite as though it had been carved with a blade. One step took us from the thick wood into the open. I took that one step and stopped, gasping, my heart pounding against my ribs.

For there, spread out before me, was War, War as I had not hoped to be able to see it, War in the open over a sunlit visible line of seven or eight miles, War spread out in a great semicircle at my very feet. Around the foot of the bare hill upon which we had so suddenly emerged curved the River Ourcq. At the left end of the visible semicircle spread out below was the city of Fère-en-Tardenois, but newly captured by the French. It was that day under heavy bombardment by the Germans. As I looked it seemed to me that the city in the valley below me was seething, boiling; that underlying it there must be volcanic action, a fire and pressure that was melting the town and breaking through the gradually liquefying crust of the place in huge upsquirting geysers of smoke and flying houses. To the immediate right of Fère-en-Tardenois, across open grain fields on the far side of the Ourcq, was the village of Seringes, then doubtfully held by our troops. Still farther to the right, across yet other open fields, was Sergy, destined for a place in American history. On the previous day American troops from a farming state of the Middle West had there met the Prussian Guard. Four times the Americans took that town with bayonet and gun butt, and four times they were driven out by the best that the Prussian army boasts. So they took it again, those American farm boys, took it and held it, and the proud Prussian Guard retired, licked to a frazzle in its first humiliating encounter with the "Idiotic Yankees." Farther yet to the right lay Cierges, still partially held by the Boche.

From Fère-en-Tardenois along the opposite bank of the Ourcq, as far to the right as I could see, the German shells were breaking. That long line of shell explosions was approximately the line of our infantry. As I saw it first it was a grotesque, billowing river of smoke and flame and uptossing earth winding through the open fields along the gentle slope on the opposite bank of the Ourcq. And all along above this crooked river of smoke and flame and dancing earth there floated slowly in the still air what first impressed me as being questing vultures. They were the compact, feathery puffs of jet-black smoke that marked the bursting shrapnel.

Beyond that first river of smoke, farther up the slope, for the most part skirting the edge of the woods on the heights, was its counterpart, a twin stream of flame and rolling smoke with the black, searching shrapnel puffs floating above. It marked the Boche line upon which the American artillery was playing. Twin rivers of death they were, flowing tumultuously along the opposite bank of the Ourcq below us there, roughly parallel. At some places they were from five to six hundred yards apart: at others not more than two hundred.

At that time I could not distinguish the individual fighting men down there in the line. I was to see them later. At first the lines were clearly marked for my eyes only by those two winding rivers of smoke and flame and flying earth.

I cannot express how naked I felt as I followed Captain X. out into that open field in plain view of the Boche lines. I felt like a scraped new skeleton hung high in the sunlit sky for the assembled world to gaze at! We were out beyond our foremost artillery, between our last guns and the line below us where the shells were breaking. In comparison to the churning sea of sound through which we had passed it seemed weirdly quiet out there in that open field.

There was the dull, hollow-sounding gro-o-o-mp of the breaking shells on the line ahead—the muffled groan and boom of the flow of those two parallel rivers of death. Behind us there was a consolidated but now somewhat distant roar of our own gun reports, and above, the constant, brassy swish of flying steel with which the field was roofed. But it seemed quiet there, and in comparison it was. Conversation in an ordinary tone was possible.

"Just what position is this, Captain X?" I inquired.

"This," he said casually, "is Hill 212!"

Hill 212! The place I couldn't reach! Misunderstanding of directions, and dumb, blind luck had brought me to the spot of spots that I wanted to reach at that particular time. The day was clear, the sun was at our backs, and the attack upon that bare slope below us was due!

The top of that bare hill upon which we stood was speckled with small shell holes until it looked liked a huge slab of Swiss cheese. They were dug by shells with instantaneous fuses which explode immediately on contact and do their biting in whatever unfortunate substance happens to be above ground rather than gouging large craters in the earth.

We walked across the top of the hill and down the slope toward the Ourcq for perhaps three or four hundred yards. There, squatted comfortably on the edge of what then seemed to me to be a fairly large shell hole, we came upon two American observers. One held a field telephone between his knees; about the neck of the other dangled a pair of observations glasses. One was industriously chewing tobacco while the other was smoking a cigarette. Both seemed bored. Squatting there on the edge of that shell hole, on that open battle field, leaning forward, elbows on knees, they reminded me of nothing so much as two life-weary small-town loafers hopelessly fishing away an afternoon from the bank of a small creek. They greeted us without surprise or enthusiasm. One allowed guardedly that it was tolerably hot down below there; the other wearily gave his opinion that everything seemed to be about the same! The captain and I knelt on the grass at the foot of a small tree some thirty feet from the shell hole and adjusted our glasses.

"See what looks like a kind of a white line down there in that open field on the other side of the river?" the captain asked, pointing. "Well, that's our infantry. They're dug in there in individual positions waiting the order to go over."

I looked and saw. There they lay, down there in that open field, beneath the flow of the river of death that the Boche artillery had loosed upon them, each man curled up in a small, hastily scooped-out hollow in the earth—waiting!

As I looked I saw a man rise from one of these small pits and, bolt upright, walk slowly along the line for perhaps twenty yards through the tossing current of that dread river, kneel down by another soldier—evidently speaking to him—and then rise and stroll back to his own scant shelter. As he walked back toward his own small pit a new sound was added to the swish of flying steel, the boom of the guns and the hollow, disgruntled gro-o-o-mp of the shells breaking on the lines.

It was the angry, simianlike staccato chattering of a machine gun: Ruppity-pup-pup! Ruppity-pup-pup-pup-pp!

"They're after him with the machine guns," the captain shouted. "Watch!"

I found watching difficult. I was so shaken with excitement that I could not hold my glasses steady at my eyes.

Why didn't that lone man walking upright down there drop flat? Why didn't he run? I suddenly found myself yelling at him to run, to hurry; foolishly shouting aloud across that stretch of battle field that they were after him, motioning for him to lie down! Seen through the powerful glasses, he seemed so near that it did not occur to me that he could not hear my voice nor see my frantic signaling.

It was only the space of a few seconds before he reached his place in the line and lay down, but it seemed to me that for hours that lone American figure was walking there in the open through that swirling dread flow under the lead hail from that savagely chattering machine gun. When he finally lay down in his place my muscles were as sore from tension as though someone had beaten me with a club!

"There they go," the captain bawled. "Off to the right there. Look!"

I looked. A little to the right there was a break in the line of recumbent figures and just in advance of that break the sunlit yellow of the open, sloping wheat field was dotted with moving brown stains. They were off!

I found myself on my feet, shaking in every limb. I remember that I was crying as I think I have never cried before, crying with excitement and an ecstatic, reverent admiration for the example of high courage that I was witnessing.

There they went, toiling along in the open up that bare slope toward a small clump of trees some three or four hundred yards ahead. And from that slump of trees there came to our ears a frantic, rattling chorus of machine-gun fire that I think more perfectly expressed fear than anything I have ever heard. The Boche was in that little clump of trees with his machine guns, fighting madly to force back that menacing, upward seepage of brown that was moving over the clear yellow of the open wheat field.

On they went! I don't see how a man lived out there, and yet while I watched I did not see a man fall! We could see the glint of their bayonets in the sun. There was one man four or five yards in advance of the rest—a lieutenant, I think—and we could see him turn every few steps and wave his men on with a gesture of his right arm.

As they approached the wood they spread out into a thin line. I saw one whole half of the line drop, and thought they had been mowed down by the fire. The other half of the line moved forward faster and suddenly dropped flat. Even as they disappeared in the wheat I saw the men on the other end of the line rise and rush. Then they dropped and those to their left rose and rushed. And so it went. They were closing in gradually on the machine guns in those woods. They were advancing now by twos, by threes, by squads in short rushes. They were out-guessing the gunners. When the fire swept to the left the men on the right rushed forward, and when the fire swept back to the right the men on the left rose and rushed.

They were in the woods! The trees hid them. We waited. It may be only imagination—probably is—but it seemed to me that at that moment I heard faintly a wild, wild exultant yell.

And then in the wheat field on the opposite side of the wood from which the Americans had entered, I saw movement again. I saw it first with the naked eye and thought it was made by our men advancing yet farther to the big wood beyond. But when I used my glasses I saw that the moving stain on the wheat field there was not brown but greenish-gray. Those moving dots were Boches, and they were running. They were the ones who had been serving the guns in that little bit of wood as our men moved up the hillside and rushed the position. And they were indeed going across that wheat field for the big wood beyond! I saw some of them go down. I saw others stop in their flight and turn, with hands high-lifted in the air, turn and walk slowly back and vanish from my sight in the wood from which they had been driven—prisoners! When I looked at the field again where the others had been running I saw no movement. And I understood the fear I had sensed in the frantic savage chattering of those machine guns in the wood as they battled to stop that upward rush of the Americans across that open field!

By this time scores of machine guns in the big wood on the crest of the slope that was held by the Boches were rattling away. All that bare slope was being swept and reswept by Boche machine guns in the big wood. And then I saw the most painfully dramatic thing I have witnessed in all this war.

Out from the little strip of wood that the Americans had just captured, walking slowly out into that open, bullet-swept field over which the charge had passed, I saw two men with the brassard of the Red Cross on their arms, bearing a wounded man on a litter. They had perhaps three hundred yards to go back across that open field before the curve of the hill would shelter them from the machine-gun fire from the hill above. And they could not run, they could not duck, they could not take cover. They must walk upright on their work of mercy, walk upright in that storm of lead, and walk slowly for the burden they bore!

"There goes two dead men," the captain said solemnly. "They haven't got a chance in that field. The machine guns'll get 'em sure. Watch!"

I watched. I have never watched anything so intently in my life. And with all the fervency of reverence and belief that there was in me I prayed for those two men of mercy over there who could not fight back; those men who had made the charge up the hill with their comrades of the gun and bayonet and must now march back bearing a wounded fighting man to safety, back through that storm of lead that was sweeping the field from the big wood—march back standing straight and walking slow. So slow!

They had made perhaps a hundred yards when one of them slipped to his knees and rolled over.

"I told you," the captain exclaimed. "They've got 'em!"

"Only one," I said. "The other fellow's not hit."

"They'll get him," the captain prophesied gloomily.

I saw the unwounded man kneel by his stricken comrade. For the space of a minute he knelt there, I suppose applying first aid. Then he stood erect. And then the man who had been hit, the stretcher bearer on the ground, rose slowly—oh, so very slowly—till he was propped up on one elbow. Then to his knees. Slow! Then very, very slowly he got to his feet. Once up, he leaned over—and, from where I was, through my glasses I could see by the movement the pain it cost—leaned over, grasped the handles of the litter, and straightened up again. He had been hit, but he was going on! On they went. I have no power to describe how slowly they seemed to be moving across that deadly open field. A hundred yards! Another hundred would mean comparative safety under the slope of the hill. Fifty of that accomplished! Twenty-five more! And then, slowly yet, they vanished from sight under the protecting slope. They had made it!

I think I shouted. I know I tried to, and I know that my knees were suddenly too weak to hold me up and that I abruptly knelt and grasped the slim bole of the little lone tree nearby to steady myself.

"There goes another bunch," the captain cried. "Off to the left there."

I saw them. They were marching up the slope to the left of the little clump of trees that had just been captured, a thin brown skirmish line, and even as I looked the Boche barrage descended on them, a great thundering fist of smoke and steel and flame driving down out of the sky.

"They're caught!" the captain groaned.

But even as that great fist crashed down, that thin line of men developed an action more swift than any I had yet seen. With one accord they turned to the left, running. I could see them leaping along through the explosions, and within the space of a minute they were out of the area upon which the barrage was descending, out of it and marching along again up the hill toward the big wood. Behind them the huge artillery fist was pounding, pounding, pounding away at an empty field.

"There goes another bunch over," the captain shouted again. "Look at 'em go! Oh, boys! Go on! Get 'em!"

They were going over everywhere all along the line. From this moment on I was in the position of a one-eyed boy trying to see everything in a three-ring circus. Wherever I looked, along that line on the far side of the Ourcq, I saw men on their way forward. The attack was on in force!

I had just steadied myself to make a systematic attempt to analyze the movement, so that I might later describe it intelligently, when I heard a wild yell from the captain.

"Beat it," he shouted. "Beat it! Beat it!"

I did! I beat it both in the slang and literal sense. Otherwise I would not be writing this. I knew what the disturbance was without asking the captain for particulars. Even my comparatively untrained ears had caught the threat of a new note in the chorus of flying steel that was passing above. It was the note made by a shell that was not flying over our heads but at them.

I think it was about thirty feet from where I was kneeling to the shell hole which was in use as an observation post. I have no recollection of getting there—but I got there! The shell and I lit at the same time. I lit in the bottom of the old shell hole, and the new shell lit precisely where the captain and I had been kneeling. It was right where we had been, but about thirty feet short of where we were.

I have a very confused recollection of the next few minutes. There were six of us tangled up in that shell hole—and what a tiny hole it was! It was one of the puniest excuses for a shell hole that I have seen on any battlefield! Really, it seemed to me that it was not a hole at all, but an eminence. The bottom of that hole felt to me like Pikes Peak on a clear day! I lay there among arms and legs, rolled into as small a lump as possible and trying to stuff all my anatomy under my tin hat. After two minutes came another shell that lit perhaps thirty feet beyond us. The first one had been short of the shell hole; the second was long!

"Boys," the captain said seriously, "we're in for it! They've got us bracketed, and we're going to get hell. Keep down as low as you can, and if any of you know any little prayers you think'll do any good, go right ahead and say 'em! Look out! Here she comes!"

She came, all right! The third was nearer than either of the first two! The fourth was nearer yet. It showered us with dirt.

"They're gettin' better all the time, aren't they?" the captain observed dryly.

They were! They just naturally sewed a ring around that shell hole. I had been shelled before, but it was the first time I had had the experience of realizing that I was a known and visible mark for a gunner to snipe at with a cannon!

We were a reasonably serious lot in that shell hole. We joked a little to show that we weren't scared—which, of course, we were—and did a little weak laughing. But it was no joke and nothing legitimate to laugh about except in retrospect. I think it was the ninth or tenth shell that for the fraction of an instant fully convinced me that I was through. The explosion turned me quite over where I lay flat there, all huddled up, and stung us all plentifully with clods. The captain told me it had exploded about ten feet away. That was close enough!

They gave us twenty shells in all at intervals of about two minutes. At the end of about forty-five or fifty minutes the captain decided that the direct salvo was over and that we might duck, one at a time. One by one we rolled out over the edge of that shell hole and went scuttling away on all fours for the nearest protection that offered, an old wall a hundred yards away. I don't know what the all-fours record for a hundred yards is, but I think I hold it. Streaking it across the field a few minutes later on the way to the road, I stopped long enough to look back and search the opposite slope where I had last seen the action. There were no moving figures to be seen in the open field, but I noted that the rivers of smoke and flame were flowing along the edge of the big wood on the crest of the slope, where before they had wound through the open fields below.

★★★

Two days later I rode over that battlefield on the far side of the Ourcq in a limousine, rode over it and for miles beyond up toward the Vesle. Those moving brown figures in the open, yellow, grain fields had done their work! They had ripped the Boche loose from his desperate grip on the heights beyond the Ourcq, and his next stopping place was miles away—in the general direction of Berlin.

★ ★ ★

William Slavens McNutt (1886–1938), was one of the motion picture industry's leading playwrights. He was not only a renowned World War I correspondent, he was also author of many magazine articles and works of fiction.

★
★
★
| OLDER MEN DECLARE WAR.
BUT IT IS THE YOUTH THAT
MUST FIGHT AND DIE. AND IT
IS YOUTH WHO MUST INHERIT
THE TRIBULATION, THE SORROW,
AND THE TRIUMPHS THAT ARE
THE AFTERMATH OF WAR.

—HERBERT CLARK HOOVER

CARRIER PIGEONS
ARE REAL HEROES

AUTHOR UNKNOWN

War heroes come in all sizes. But who would even dream that some of them would wear feathers!

In World War I, since electronic communication was still in its infancy, soldiers in emergencies often felt doomed, knowing it was virtually impossible to get news of their plight to rescuers in time. Well, a British seaplane crashed into the North Sea, and was slowly sinking. There was only one hope: a very wet and chilled little pigeon.

This is the story.

★ ★ ★

Try to imagine yourself clinging to the half-submerged wreck of a seaplane out in the North Sea fifteen miles from shore, wet to the skin, chilled to the bone, and desperately weary. Hours before, you had released a homing pigeon with a message calling for help, and you hate to admit how little faith you have in its reaching its loft at all, against the wind and rain, let alone in time to be of any use to you. Yet you know it is your *only* chance. Night is coming on, and if that bird has not reached its home, your name will be published in the next casualty list.

Then as your hope is dying, and you are trying to behave as brave men should, a lean greyhound of a motorboat comes racing up out of the fog. As you are taken aboard to warmth and dry clothes and food—to life and all that life holds dear, you are told that the ship was sent in response to a message brought by the little homing pigeon, which was almost dead from exhaustion as it entered the trap. You will have something new to think about. You may not have much sentiment; you may not be interested in bird conservation, but it is pretty certain that unless the North Sea has washed all the decency out of you, you will walk a long way to vote against live-pigeon shooting the next chance you get.

As you may suppose, the pigeon used as a war messenger was not the ordinary variety commonly seen on the barns in country places, but a special breed which originated in Belgium, and which was developed chiefly in Liège, Verviers, Brussels, and Antwerp. It is the only pigeon capable of homing from very long distances. Although during the war and at other times it has been referred to as the "carrier" pigeon, the "carrier" is an entirely different breed, which long ago came from Baghdad, and which in the early days of pigeon racing in England was used for short-distance flights up to one hundred miles. The homing pigeon was used by the French with great effect during the Siege of Paris, 1870–71, and soon thereafter the English fanciers got in touch with Belgium, and the "homer" was at once replaced with birds then used for racing purposes—the "carrier," the "horseman," and a cross between these two, known as the "dragon." Because of the use to which it is put in peace times, it is now generally spoken of among English pigeon flyers as the "racing" pigeon.

The marvelous homing instinct of these birds, known also as the "instinct of orientation," has been the subject of much study. They are extremely sensitive, and their powers are by no means equal. It is probable that this great sensitiveness enables the bird to perceive magnetic and atmospheric impressions, and to determine the direction of the loft, either at the time of departure or when, during flight, he may have lost his way, owing to unexpected variations in the weather. As is the case with the training of all animals, it is the men who have these delicate organisms in their care, and the necessary intelligence, firmness, patience, and love, who are responsible for their development, their usefulness, and their success.

Racing pigeons, by reason of this strong desire to return to their homes, their splendid powers of flight (they have been known to fly for fifteen continuous hours), and their remarkable memory for places, may be trained to fly great distances to definite points—the points at which their lofts are stationed. Many pigeons have flown five hundred miles, some have records of seven to eight hundred miles, and a very few have actually come back one thousand miles or more. But such birds are the best athletes of their breed, and their performances are usually made under the most favorable conditions which can be arranged for them.

The question of good communication is one of the most important in modern warfare, especially during actual fighting. The vast number of men engaged, the wide territory over which they are distributed, the interdependence of artillery, infantry, cavalry, tanks, air forces, and other branches of the service, and especially the distances which often separate the fighters from the men who are directing the fighting, make it imperative that commanding officers be kept informed of what is going on at the many points which are at once involved.

The shells of a particular battery are not finding their mark. The observation officer far ahead of the guns must notify the gunmen in order that the aim may be corrected. A certain part of the line is weak, and needs reinforcements. That information must be sent to some officer having power to send up the relief. A battalion has advanced too far, and has been cut off by the enemy. It can be saved only if troops are sent forward promptly. The fate of that battalion depends upon the ability of its commander to communicate quickly with someone having the reserve troops, and the authority to send them.

In short, the winning of a great battle may depend upon a single message reaching its destination on time. So very important, then, was a reliable system of communication. Many were the agencies employed. Among them were the telephone, ground and wireless telegraph, signal lantern, luminous signals, messenger dogs, mounted couriers, runners, scout detachments, and aviators. Each one of these was useful, each had its special advantages, but there were times and places when a single homing pigeon, flying a mile a minute and knowing exactly where it was going was worth all of them put together.

Messages were attached to birds in various ways. The commonest, and perhaps the best, was by means of a pair of small aluminum tubes, which snugly fitted one into the other, like sections of a telescope, forming a capsule, or cylinder, closed at both ends. The tube having the slightly larger diameter was fastened by metal bands, mouth-upward, to the leg of the pigeon; the smaller one, containing the message, was then pushed into the larger, mouth downward. The Italians sometimes used a very small chamois leather envelope, which, after receiving the message, was buttoned around the leg of the bird. In emergencies, the message was simply wrapped around the pigeon's leg, and secured by two ordinary rubber bands. When unusually long messages, sketches, or maps were sent, they were put in a light cloth knapsack made to fit the rounded breast of the bird, and held in position by elastic bands which circled the body, crossing on the back. Sometimes as much as fifteen feet of moving-picture-film negative was carried by a pigeon in this way.

If a pigeon was released in good condition, failure to return to the loft was usually due to death from poison gas or enemy fire. But so long as the wings were not badly injured, it was a desperate wound indeed that prevented a homing pigeon from delivering his message. The loss of a leg or an eye was quite a common occurrence, and such an injury in itself was not enough to prevent the bird from finishing the task it had been sent to do.

In our own American Army there were several pigeons that distinguished themselves by delivering messages in spite of terrible wounds. Probably the best known of them all is Cher Ami, the black checker cock that delivered twelve important messages on the Verdun front, and at last lost a leg in the Argonne. His story has been often told, but will bear repeating. The little courier was hit by a bullet just as he was leaving Grand Pré. The boys in the trenches watched him stagger, and shouted, "He's done for!" and watched to see where he would fall, but he didn't fall. For a few seconds he fluttered helplessly about, then gathering himself together, he went on through the hail of bullets and machine-gun fire, and was out of sight.

No one can tell what Cher Ami passed through on that awful, terrible flight over the hills to his home. But suddenly above his loft at Ramot he appears again, and drops from the sky like a rocket. Striking the loft, breast first, he staggers, sways from side to side, and then, hopping on one bloody leg, he makes for the entrance landing board, where he is received by his trainer. The tube bearing the message was hanging by the ligaments of the leg that had been shot through; there was a hole through the breast bone made by the same bullet. But for all that, Cher Ami had covered his twenty-five miles in as many minutes.

★ ★ ★

It was late in the afternoon. One of England's largest seaplanes had just completed a long antisubmarine patrol above the North Sea, and her tired pilot gladly swung her around and headed for his base. Then something went wrong. The huge craft plunged downward, righted itself, plunged again, and dived sideways into the water. There was an ominous cracking and ripping, some quick, dangerous work by the crew, and four men stood upon a wrecked and wave-swept seaplane. How long she would float, heavily laden as she was with motor and armament, none could tell, but what every man did know was that help must come quickly from somewhere, or it need not come at all.

Then somebody shouted, "The pigeons!" A dripping basket was found and opened, but alas, two of the three birds were dead, and the survivor was so wet and chilled that its recovery was doubtful. But it seemed the only chance, and an officer wrapped it in a woolen muffler which, by some miracle was dry, and placed the bundle inside his shirt. In half an hour the pigeon had somewhat revived, and as the daylight was already failing, it was decided to wait no longer. A brief message was written, rolled up, and pushed into a small aluminum cylinder, and the cylinder was attached to the right leg of the bird.

It was an anxious moment when the pilot climbed to a high point on the wreck and tossed the little messenger into the air. It fell, and every heart sank with it. Then, catching itself just above the waves, it lifted itself a little. For several seconds it barely held its own, then seeming to gain strength by its own effort, it rose slowly, squared away, and disappeared in the battleship gray.

Somewhere on the northeast coast of England night was approaching under a drizzly mist, and a raw wind whipped land and sea around the lonely group of buildings known as "Royal Air Force Pigeon Station No. _____." It was tea time, and a welcome hour to the little group of bronzed "noncoms" and men in British uniform who were chatting and laughing around the small fire in the mess room.

Suddenly the laugh which greeted a story was cut in two by a sound which caused every man in the room to pause and listen. It was the sharp, insistent call of the electric bell that rings automatically when a homing pigeon enters the "trap." A noncommissioned officer set down his cup of tea untasted, arose, and opened the door leading to the pigeon loft. From a corner where it had huddled, he lifted a light blue pigeon, very wet and bedraggled, skillfully removed a small aluminum cylinder from its right leg, slipped the bird into a pigeon basket, and carried it into the mess room, where he set it on the warm hearth and drew from the little cylinder a roll of tissue paper, smoothed it out flat, and read aloud:

"Machine wrecked and breaking up fifteen miles southeast of Rocky Point. Send boat."

Two men had already reached for their oilskins, and were passing out of the door into the fog. Another minute and the staccato "put-put-put" of a motor boat was heard dying away in the general direction of Rocky Point.

Darkness had fallen on the North Sea, and four men, wet and chilled, still clung to the wrecked seaplane. They had little hope that their message had been delivered, or if it had been, that help would come in time to save them. The wind had risen, and now and then the waves tore some portion of the wreck, which sank lower and lower in the water. At last there came a sound, the sweetest music they had ever heard—the siren of a motor boat. Again and again it sounded, each time nearer; then the heartened men arose and sent up a wild shout in answer, and a hissing bow shot toward them from the darkness.

On the top of a little basket by the fire in the mess room a modest blue pigeon sat quietly preening its damp feathers. And the next morning the British papers reported:

"Seaplane 'N-64' lost in the North Sea, fifteen miles southeast of Rocky Point. *All the crew were saved.*"

★
★
★

My duty is to obey orders.

—THOMAS JONATHAN "STONEWALL" JACKSON

HOW THE BRITISH SANK
THE *SCHARNHORST*

C. S. FORESTER

I t was the twilight of an era, though no one then suspected it. During the war years of the thirties and forties, ironclad floating fortresses ruled the waves. In them men, engines, oil, armor, and artillery struggled, massive and deadly, for mastery of the sea lanes. This eyewitness account, written by then-war-correspondent C. S. Forester, best known for the great *Hornblower* sea novels, has been called "the best piece of naval reporting to come out of World War II."

★ ★ ★

In those almost forgotten days when there were pleasure cruises, we used to see posters advertising trips to "The Land of the Midnight Sun." Of course, those were summer cruises; if any steamship company had been so foolish as to try to induce people to go to North Cape in winter, they would have had to advertise "The Land of the

66

★SOLDIER STORIES

Midday Night." On December 26th in those latitudes, seventy-five degrees north, the sun never comes above the horizon, and it is poor compensation to know it is circling not far below the horizon.

In ordinary weather it is never pitch dark. At noon it is a pale gray, and from noon it darkens imperceptibly until at midnight everything is dark gray. On a fair proportion of days and nights the green-and-yellow streamers of the aurora borealis give a fitful and erratic illumination. But there are just as many nights when the wind blows down from the Pole, tearing the tormented sea into lumpy mountains and engulfing the world in flurries of snow, so that the black sky gives no light and one cannot, literally, see one's hand before one's face.

Those are the times when it is not well to be a lookout, shivering in ten thicknesses of wool inside a sheepskin coat. The depth charges freeze to the decks; the breeches of the guns are covered with ice—unless precautions are taken—so that the breech-blocks cannot be opened; the lubrication of the ammunition hoists freezes solid. No ship can fight a battle in those wintry waters without special accessories for keeping the weapons clear of ice and for keeping life in the officers and men, wedged so that they can hardly move in the exposed gunnery-control stations.

It is through these waters that the lifeline runs to Russia. The heavy convoys, laden with all the innumerable materials of war from the mines and factories of the world, make their way to Murmansk round the most northerly point of Norway. The farther north they keep, the longer is the journey they must make, at a time when even hours are important; the stormier are the seas they meet, and the greater are their chances of encountering ice. The farther south they keep, the quicker they make their run—and the more exposed they are to German attacks launched from Norway, above the surface of the sea, on the surface of the sea, and below the surface of the sea.

Attacks by airplane and by submarine, in present technical conditions, however, can only harass the convoys and not stop them. There is only one thing that could stop them, in fact, and that is superior sea power. If Germany had a fleet more powerful than that of the United Nations, not a convoy would move on the high seas, not a single ship, save for occasional furtive blockade runners. But Germany does not have a superior fleet; she has a very inferior one. If the inferior fleet fights, it is destroyed. If it stays at home, it yields free use of the sea to the enemy, and might as well never have been built.

Between the two horns of this dilemma the weaker naval powers have always tried to find a profitable middle course. If the weaker power has a secure base within striking distance of the trade routes, the presence of its fleet there imposes certain troublesome precautions on the stronger power. It offers the threat of sallying out at a moment of its own selection, so that every convoy moved by the superior power must be guarded by a force greater than the whole fleet of the inferior power, and that necessarily involves strain and potential loss—the strain of staying at sea and of replacing the oil fuel consumed, and the losses from submarines and from the hazards of the sea.

But the threat must always be a real one. The weaker fleet must come out sometimes or it will find itself simply ignored. Moreover, mutinies breed readily in stagnant fleets, especially when the best of the men are steadily drained away for the submarine service. And even in a guarded base things can happen, as when the British midget submarines crept in and torpedoed the *Tirpitz*.

It was this loss which must have roused the Nazi government to desperation. The Russian offensive was rolling along unchecked. Something must be done at all costs to check the flow of supplies to her, before something should happen to the *Scharnhorst* as well. The *Tirpitz* was a wreck, only kept afloat by the constant attention of a salvage ship; the *Gneisenau* was in even worse condition at Gdynia.

The *Spee* and the *Bismarck* had been sunk. Of Germany's twenty-six destroyers, eleven were at the other end of Europe, waiting to bring in a blockade runner from the east. The Nazis could not foresee that in less than a week they would be foiled in their object and three of them sent to the bottom, and the blockade runner along with them. The straggling remainder of Germany's navy was in the Baltic, for the possibility of the loss of the command of that sea to the Russian navy was something too horrible to contemplate.

Maybe the Nazis knew about the presence of that convoy to the north of North Cape. Maybe a U-boat had sighted it and had radioed information of its position and course. Maybe some unguarded word spoken in a British port may have told a Nazi spy what he wanted to know. Maybe the *Scharnhorst* was sent out into the Arctic night on the mere chance of striking against something. At any rate, out she went from her Norwegian fiord, wearing at her masthead the flag—a black cross and two black balls on a white ground—of Rear Admiral Bey, commanding German destroyers.

For the purposes of a raid she had all the desirable qualities. Designed for a speed of twenty-nine knots, she was faster—or so, at least, the Nazis hoped—than any British battleship. With nine 11-inch guns she was more powerful than any British cruiser; with her displacement of twenty-six thousand tons she carried sufficient armor and was sufficiently compartmented to be able to receive a number of hard knocks without being crippled. And her enormous secondary armament of twelve 5.9-inch guns and fourteen 4.1s would insure that if she once got into a convoy she would sink ships faster than a fox killing chickens in a hen-roost.

At her high speed she could cover the whole distance in darkness, leaving her Norwegian fiord at the end of twilight one day and arriving in the area through which a convoy would be likely to pass at the beginning of twilight the next, so that she could be firing shells into helpless merchantmen before any British plane or submarine could detect her absence or catch a glimpse of her on passage. For closely associated reasons she had no destroyer escort; destroyers are running short in the Nazi navy; to give orders for destroyers to join her would give an additional chance for the Intelligence of the United Nations to get wind of the scheme; and, above all, a German ship steaming by herself on the high seas has the supreme advantage of the certainty that anything she sights is an enemy—she can open fire instantly, without having to wait for challenge and recognition.

She left on the afternoon of Christmas Day [1943], and such was her good fortune or so accurate was her information that at precisely the right time, just when the gloomy northern sea was beginning to be faintly illumined and the dark gray of the sky was being replaced by something the merest trifle brighter, she made her contact with the convoy. There was any amount of shipping there, anything up to half a million tons. It was possible for her, in the next hour, to do as much damage as the whole U-boat navy could achieve in six months. In an hour she could put back the hands of the clock of war by four weeks.

At 9:30 in the morning of the day after Christmas, the British convoy was heading east some one hundred fifty miles to the northward of North Cape. It was guarded against submarine attack by a ring of corvettes and destroyers, small craft, twenty of which together would hardly equal the *Scharnhorst* in size. That was the antisubmarine protection; to guard against attack by surface vessels, Admiral Burnett had three cruisers, *Belfast, Norfolk,* and *Sheffield.* The southeast was the most dangerous quarter, from which attack was most likely to come, so that it was to the southeast of the convoy that Burnett had stationed his squadron, and it was from the southeast that Bey arrived.

It could not be called bad luck that the *Scharnhorst*'s first contact was made with the escort instead of with the helpless merchant ships. She could expect nothing else, for the British cruisers and destroyers covering the convoy must be disposed in a manner to guard against any possible attack. It might be considered possible for her, with all the advantage of surprise, to crash through the screen and plunge in among the unarmed ships which were her real objective. It would be dangerous, for there is great danger in approaching too close to an enemy who is still in a condition to launch torpedoes. Bey had hardly more than seconds in which to make up his mind whether he should make the attempt. The *Scharnhorst* and the British escort sighted each other at six miles. A thousand yards short of that distance, decisive torpedo range begins, and battleship and escort hurtling together would close the range by one thousand yards in less than a minute.

Aboard the British ships, the unsleeping eye which all United Nations ships carry—the eye that can see in the dark, can see through the Arctic night, through fog or snowstorm—had been watching over their safety. It had given the first alarm, and now was reporting to bridge and to gunnery-control tower just where this intruder, this almost certain enemy, was to be found and whither she was headed. The guns were training round in accordance with its observations, and the gunnery officers in their control towers were eying the "gun-ready" lamps and awaiting the moment to open fire.

It was as if the shepherd's dogs, guarding the flock, had scented the approach of the wolf, and had rushed forward to put themselves between the wolf and the flock, baying the warning which the mast-head signal lamps sent through the twilight to the commodore of the convoy. Ponderously, in obedience to the commodore's orders, the convoy turned itself about—not an easy thing to do with heavy columns of unhandy merchant ships—while the *Norfolk*, the *Sheffield* and the *Belfast* went dashing forward to meet the enemy.

In a broadside or in a given interval of time, the *Scharnhorst* could fire rather more than the weight of shells that could be fired by the three cruisers all put together. It would be a fortunate light cruiser that could sustain a hit from one of the 11-inch shells of the *Scharnhorst* and live through it. The armor that the *Scharnhorst* carried over her vitals could be relied upon to keep out the cruisers' shells at all but the closest range. Mathematically, the approaching conflict was to the last degree unfair.

Yet in war at sea mathematics plays, even in these days of machinery, only a minor part. There are the discipline and training of the crews to be taken into account, the experience and resolution of the captains, and, above all, there is chance—the chance that will take a ship unscathed through a hail of salvos, the chance that will direct a shell to the one point where it will rend a ship in two, the chance that will direct a desperate torpedo to its mark.

The three cruisers flung themselves upon the *Scharnhorst*. Twenty-six thousand tons tearing through a rough sea at thirty knots displace a prodigious amount of water. Even though in that gloomy twilight—9:30 a.m., and very little light creeping round the curve of the earth as yet—the glittering white bow wave flung up by the *Scharnhorst* could be seen even when her gray upper works were invisible. A gun was fired in the British squadron and a star shell traced a lovely curve of white light through the twilight before it burst fairly over the battle cruiser, lighting up her and the sea for a mile around her more brightly than any winter noontime in those latitudes. It hung in the sky like the Star of Bethlehem at another Christmas-tide as its parachute sustained it in the air seemingly without falling at all, and, as it hung, the cruisers' guns opened fire on the target.

The shells went screaming on their mission—long range for 6-inch, only medium range for 11-inch—and the spotting officer of the *Norfolk*, staring through his glasses, saw, just at that very second when the *Norfolk*'s shells should land, a vivid green flash from the *Scharnhorst*'s black hull. The *Norfolk* carried 8-inch guns—the other cruisers only 6-inch—and there was a chance—although not a very big one—that the *Scharnhorst* might be badly hurt.

The *Scharnhorst* spun about so rapidly that the next salvo fell harmlessly into the sea where she would have been had she maintained her course, and dashed out of the illuminated circle. When ships are six miles apart and traveling at a combined speed of sixty miles an hour, touch is broken as quickly as it can be made. She vanished into the twilight.

Bey is dead now. We do not know, and very likely we never shall know, what were the motives that induced him to turn away. It is just possible that he was deterred by the sight of the three British cruisers flinging themselves upon him like a trio of wildcats—possible but hardly probable. It is not likely that a man could rise to admiral's rank in the Nazi navy if he were of the stuff that flinches. The hit that the Norfolk scored may have caused enough damage to force him to turn, but it takes time—several seconds, if not more—for details of damage to be ascertained and reported to the bridge, and it seems certain that the *Scharnhorst* turned away the moment she was hit.

Most likely, Bey was acting on a plan he had devised long beforehand. It was the convoy he was after. He did not want to fight ships of war and risk damage to his precious battleship unless circumstances compelled him to do so. If he stayed and fought it out with the three cruisers, there was a chance that the *Scharnhorst* might be hit and crippled; in another two minutes there would be eighteen torpedoes launched from the cruisers' decks and hurtling toward him, and any one of those might slow him up enough to incapacitate him. He thought the odds were not profitable in terms of the stake, and he withdrew.

He knew now where were the main defenses of the convoy, and he could guess with some accuracy where the merchant ships themselves were to be found. He could circle away, losing himself in the gloom, and then, turning back, he could make a fresh stab which ought to slip past the British guard.

Admiral Burnett was in command of the British cruiser force, with his flag flying on the *Belfast*. A sailor of vast experience, this was by no means the first convoy which he had escorted to Murmansk. But now he was presented with no mere problem of navigation or seamanship. No rule of thumb could be of the least assistance to him in this present situation. What he had to do was to guess what Bey would do next. Anybody could be quite certain that Bey's one aim was to get in among the merchant ships, but to guess where and when he would make his attack was something that was far more difficult to foresee.

A thirty-knot battleship tearing through the gloom could sweep in an hour all round the convoy at a distance which would make her safe from detection, even by the instruments which the British ships carried. It would take the *Scharnhorst* no more than five minutes to come in over the horizon within range of the merchant vessels and no more than five minutes after that, as has already been said, to wipe out a month's efforts by all the factories in the world. So there was no margin whatever for miscalculation on the part of the British; Burnett had to put himself in the path of the *Scharnhorst*'s next attack, and that attack might come from north or east or west or south.

If it should come from the east when Burnett was in the west, the British cruisers might as well be in the Pacific for any protection they could give to the merchant ships. It was not a question of having to guess which of two possible courses Bey would adopt; it was a question of guessing which of some sixteen courses. Burnett had to guess within a very few degrees on what bearing Bey would reappear over the horizon, and he had to have his cruisers there. It was strictly his problem—a one-man decision. The staff at the Admiralty, reading off the scrappy wireless intercepts, might be able to offer him advice, but they could not relieve him of the responsibility. He had a purely intellectual problem to solve as he stood on the crowded and exposed bridge, with the spray flying aft as the Belfast tore at top speed over the heaving sea.

He solved it. It was 9:30, the beginning of the winter day, when the *Scharnhorst* made her first contact with the cruisers from the southeast. At 12:30—high noon—the *Scharnhorst* reappeared from the northeast, to find Burnett and his cruisers right in her path. It was an extraordinary achievement on Burnett's part, seeing that the *Scharnhorst* could have appeared anywhere along the circumference of a circle of at least two thousand one hundred miles; her speed, well over twice that of the convoy, gave her, of course, complete liberty of action. What Bey thought of this extraordinary apparition of three indomitable cruisers right in his path when by all the laws of chance they should have been twenty miles away can be guessed from his actions. There was a sudden flurry of salvos, during which a single shell landed and burst on the *Norfolk*'s stern, and then Bey turned and ran for home.

It was dangerous for him to stay out longer. Three hours had elapsed since the British had first become aware that the *Scharnhorst* was out. It would take another hour or two, at least, of maneuvers if he were to make another attempt to strike at the convoy without fighting his way through, and the arguments against fighting his way through were as cogent now as they had been three hours earlier. He did not wish to risk being cut off from his base, and if he headed for home now, he had just sufficient time to reach his protecting fiord before next morning's daylight. He could not doubt that three hours ago, the moment Burnett first sighted him, hurried messages had been broadcast to the British Admiralty and to the main British fleet; nor could he doubt that the British were at this moment straining every nerve to send ships and aircraft to guard their precious convoy and to attack a ship as valuable as the *Scharnhorst*.

As a matter of fact, there was far more risk than he knew. One hundred and fifty miles to the southwest of him, and steaming fast to cut him off, was a force which could make scrap iron of his ship. This was the *Duke of York* with her attendant cruiser, the *Jamaica*, and her screen of four destroyers. From her masthead flew the St. George's cross of a full admiral—no less a person than Sir Bruce Fraser, commander in chief of the Home Fleet. Nobody outside a few favored persons knew how many times the patient Royal Navy had set that trap, how many times a battleship force had plodded along from England to Russia on a course parallel to, but well away from, that of the convoy, in the hope of intercepting any Nazi force sent out from Norway. Probably it had been done over and over again, and this was the first time that patience and resolution were to be rewarded.

Fraser, in the *Duke of York*, was about two hundred miles away from the convoy when, at 9:30, came Burnett's first message of the appearance of the *Scharnhorst*. There would have been nothing gained, and the risk of much being lost, if he had been any nearer. The wary and elusive enemy had an advantage in speed of several knots. Fraser had to be sure of being able to interpose between the *Scharnhorst* and her base; any mere pursuit was doomed to failure before it started.

Not that there was any certainty about cutting the enemy off from his base. The sea is wide and the Arctic night can be intense. Unless Fraser was able to place himself squarely across the *Scharnhorst's* path, there was every chance that she would slip past him. Hence during that Sunday morning while Burnett was wondering where the *Scharnhorst* would reappear, Fraser was having to decide upon his own course of action. He sent his men to action stations, and at increased speed he and his cruiser and destroyers headed toward the strategical center of gravity—the nearest point of a straight line between the *Scharnhorst's* last known position and the German base.

In the British battleship, as in every other ship, the only men who moved from their posts during that day were those sent down to the galleys to fetch their comrades' dinners. It was a Sunday dinner—soup, pork chops and baked potatoes—and this the men ate at their posts, squatting on the heaving decks, jammed closely in turrets and shell rooms or swaying about in the gunnery-control towers one hundred feet above the surface of the sea.

Dinner had hardly been eaten in these uncomfortable circumstances when the next flash of news came from Burnett; the *Scharnhorst* had made her second appearance, and Fraser now knew her exact position again. She was still one hundred fifty miles away, Fraser was nearer to her base than she was, but it was certain that contact would only be made—if it was made at all—in three or four hours' time, long after twilight had ceased.

It was time for Burnett to distinguish himself again. The *Scharnhorst*, after scoring her hit on the *Norfolk*, had headed south through the twilight. Burnett swung his ships to starboard in pursuit. It was of the utmost importance that Fraser should be kept informed of the *Scharnhorst*'s course and position, so that he could place himself to meet her as she came down from the north. Burnett had to keep in touch with the *Scharnhorst*, but to keep in touch with a ship that mounts nine 11-inch guns is more easily asked than done. Those 11-inch guns were capable of hitting a target clean over the horizon, farther than the eye could see, and it needed only one of those salvos, landing square, to smash any one of the frail cruisers into a sinking wreck.

During that anxious afternoon the listeners at the Admiralty took in message after message which told them of how Burnett was maintaining contact, and on their charts they could prick off the *Scharnhorst*'s position as she came nearer to the safety of the Norwegian coast. They knew that somewhere in that neighborhood was the commander in chief, steering steadily eastward in grim wireless silence. So far, he had done nothing to reveal his position, for he knew perfectly well that a score of stations in Norway and Germany were eagerly taking in every message that passed over the ether, even if they were unable to decipher them. One whisper from the *Duke of York*'s radio and the direction-finding stations would locate it instantly, and the transmitting stations would flash the news to the *Scharnhorst* of the presence of another British force—strength unknown, but obviously to be avoided—to the southward of him. But the Germans did not know Fraser was at sea; Bey did not know; and although Burnett and the Admiralty knew he was at sea, they did not know where he was. They could only hope.

Then all doubts were suddenly resolved in one glorious moment. The *Duke of York* broke her wireless silence, and the message which the Admiralty listeners took in was an order from Fraser to Burnett to "illuminate the enemy with star shell." Then they knew that Fraser's calculated position was very close to the position which Burnett was reporting for the Scharnhorst. The *Duke of York*'s navigating officers had done a neat professional job. Counting every turn of their ship's propellers, making allowance for current and wind, they had fixed their own position accurately on the chart. At the same time they had deduced from Burnett's reports what was the *Scharnhorst*'s course and what would be her present position. Burnett's navigators had been equally brilliant, for they could only report the *Scharnhorst*'s position with reference to their own calculated position. It should be remembered that at Jutland in World War I, over distances not nearly so great, Jellicoe and Beatty miscalculated their relative positions with a total error of seven miles and serious results to Jellicoe's deployment. An error of seven miles in the present circumstances would give the *Scharnhorst* every chance of dashing by unharmed.

It was 4:30, quite dark, when Fraser broke wireless silence and the warning gong sounded in the *Duke of York*. The *Scharnhorst* was on his port bow, and the *Belfast* was eight miles astern of the *Scharnhorst*. Before the *Scharnhorst*'s wireless telegraphists, having heard the *Duke of York* signaling, could have communicated to Bey on the bridge the appalling news of an enemy close ahead, the fifth act of the tragedy—played throughout in the dark, like *Macbeth*—

had begun. A streak of white fire shot from one of the *Belfast*'s guns and soared against the black sky, eight miles in twenty seconds. The shell burst high up, with a faint report unnoticeable in the blustery night, and then the tremendous white flare blazed out, sinking slowly under its supporting parachute and lighting up the scene over a two-mile radius.

Right in the center of that blaze of white light was the *Scharnhorst*, and the lookouts and spotters and gunnery officers in Fraser's force saw her upper works brightly lit, standing out boldly against the horizon. The rating at the director sight trained his instrument upon her; the 14-inch guns moved their thousands of tons of dead weight round in obedience to its dictation, and when the gunnery officer said "Open fire," five 14-inch guns roared out with the incredibly loud din of their kind and sent three and a half tons of shells—three and a half tons of hot steel and high explosive—at their mark. For a score of seconds the shells rumbled through the air; one of the destroyers in the *Duke of York*'s screen under the arch of their trajectory heard them pass overhead like maddened express trains.

Then they landed, flinging up their two-hundred-foot splashes under the unearthly illumination of the star shell. So closely had the range been estimated that this first salvo was registered as a "straddle," with some shells falling this side of the mark and some the other. And the next salvo, following less than half a minute later, recorded a hit. At least one shell, of three quarters of a ton weight, had struck home on the *Scharnhorst*, so that there were Germans on board who were killed without even knowing of the sudden dramatic appearance of a British battleship on the *Scharnhorst*'s starboard bow.

Chance dictated that she should be struck without being disabled. Half a minute elapsed between the moment when the *Duke of York* was illuminated by the blaze of fire from her gun muzzles and the moment when the *Scharnhorst* staggered under the titanic blow of the striking shell; that half minute was long enough for Bey to grasp the implications of those gun flashes on the horizon and to give the order which spun the *Scharnhorst's* wheel hard aport and sent her wildly seeking safety in the eastward darkness.

The *Scharnhorst* sped eastward with every revolution her engineers could wring from her turbines, and after her came the British ships. There was still hope, for Bey knew he had an advantage of several knots in speed over any British battleship. In two hours' flight he could be out of range, and in darkness and at those colossal speeds there was nothing fantastic in hoping that his ship would avoid fatal injury for that time—to say nothing of the fact that his own fire might disable his enemy first. He turned his stern square to his pursuer, thereby at the same time presenting the smallest possible target and making the best use of his difference of speed, and he trained aft those of his guns that would bear, fired a star shell, and began a methodical return fire upon the *Duke of York*.

His hope of hitting the *Duke of York* on her water line or in her engines, and thereby slowing her down, came to nothing, but one of his shells scored a hit which might have proved equally important. Fragments struck the mast, and one of them cut away the wireless aerial. By that stroke the commander in chief of the Home Fleet was sundered from communication with the rest of the world and was rendered unable either to coordinate the action of the four cruisers and the four destroyers under his command or to report his position and progress. Had the *Duke of York* remained unable to give orders to the destroyers, the *Scharnhorst* might possibly have survived. But Lt. H. R. J. Bates effected a temporary repair in the quickest possible way. He climbed the mast—in the dark, with the wind whipping round him and the ship lurching fantastically over the waves—and he held the ends of the aerial together for the orders to pass. Eleven-inch shells were being fired at the ship while he did so, and the splashes from near misses rose to his level.

The *Scharnhorst* survived the broadsides of the *Duke of York* for more than an hour, and although she was hit and hit again, she was not wounded sufficiently to make any immediate difference to her speed. The time interval had been long enough for her to increase her distance from the *Duke of York* by at least five miles, and before half past six she was out of range, battered, on fire, but safe from the *Duke of York* for the moment. But hardly had the exasperated gunnery officer in the *Duke of York* given the word to cease fire when a new blaze of gunfire lit the horizon far ahead where the Scharnhorst had last been seen. She was having to defend herself against new enemies.

The four destroyers of the *Duke of York*'s screen, *Savage*, *Saumarez*, *Scorpion* and *Stord*—the last a vessel of the Norwegian navy—found themselves, when the action began between the two battleships, ahead of the *Duke of York* and astern of the *Scharnhorst*. Their superiority of speed enabled them to head-reach upon the *Scharnhorst* even while the *Scharnhorst* was drawing away from the *Duke of York*. The *Savage* and *Saumarez* overhauled her on the starboard side, the *Scorpion* and *Stord* on her port side. In that hour and a half they were able to sweep right around her and then dash in, two on either bow—torpedo attacks, to be effective, must be launched from ahead of the target.

The attacks were made in the nick of time, just as the *Scharnhorst* escaped from the battleship's guns. The *Scharnhorst* saw them and opened fire with all the innumerable guns of her secondary battery, but destroyers charging in at forty knots from opposite sides are hard to stop. Moreover, she had been hard hit by half a dozen heavy shells, with the almost certain result of damage to her guns and system of communications.

It seems that at this very moment her speed suddenly fell to twenty knots as a result of injuries inflicted on her by the *Duke of York*'s guns; at a guess, a condenser had been damaged and a boiler eventually put out of action by the entrance of salt water. From a spectacular point of view, her defense was dramatic enough. She was one vast glow from the orange-red flames of her guns, and from this central nucleus radiated the innumerable streaks of tracer shells—tracers that she was firing at the destroyers and tracers which every ship arriving in range fired back at her.

Yet her fire was singularly ineffective. Only the *Saumarez* was hit, and although the damage to the destroyer's upper works resulted in regrettable casualties, her fighting value was not greatly impaired. The destroyers pressed home their attack to the uttermost limit. They did not loose their torpedoes at the ten-thousand-yard range which is the torpedo's maximum, nor at six thousand yards, which experience has shown to be the nearest a destroyer can hope to approach a well-defended capital ship. They pressed in to two thousand yards and less, launched their torpedoes, and then, with their wheels hard over, sheered away from the doomed battleship.

Several of the torpedoes—how many there is no means of knowing—struck home, but the battle flared up with even greater violence. One singular advantage which the German navy has always possessed was clearly demonstrated at this crisis. As the weaker naval power, she has never had to design her ships for ability to keep the sea for long periods of time; swift and sudden blows were all she expected of them, with the result that habitability is not considered a necessity. They can lie in harbor with their crews on shore in barracks most of the time, so that they can be compartmented in a fashion impossible to British or American ships. The *Scharnhorst* survived these several underwater blows and maintained a tremendous volume of fire, comparatively ill-directed but impressive.

With the *Scharnhorst* falling off in speed, the *Duke of York* came up in range again, and the 14-inch guns began to smash her to pieces. At the same time every British ship closed in and opened fire. The *Duke of York*'s attendant cruiser, *Jamaica*, which had been firing intermittently during the whole easterly run, drew up on one side of her to use her 6-inch guns at point-blank range. Burnett and his three cruisers pressed in on the other, and the wretched ship, unable any longer to keep her fires under control, blazed out in a sudden volcano of flame even while she maintained her return fire, dropping several shells close to the *Duke of York*.

Nor were these her only assailants, for there now arrived on the scene four more destroyers, part of the convoy escort, who, having made sure that no other enemy was likely to attack their charges, came dashing down with proper military instinct to where the battle was taking place. There was danger of effort being wasted by all this concentration of force. It is impossible for gunfire to be properly directed when several ships are firing on one target in uncoordinated fashion. In the pitch darkness no fewer than eight destroyers, four cruisers and a battleship were tearing about at their highest speed round the *Scharnhorst*. Torpedoes were being launched and guns were being fired by eager captains anxious to be in at the kill. British fighting blood was aflame. Hotheads might be carried away by their own enthusiasm, and it was time for the master hand to take control again. The signal sent out by the commander in chief can be given in its entirety because, owing to the urgency of the occasion, it was in plain English, so publication gives the Nazis no chance of breaking the British code.

The message was perfectly calm and methodical, betraying no sign of the excitement of the moment. "Clear the area of the target," it said, "except for those ships with torpedoes and one destroyer with searchlight." It was like the bugles blowing for the death of a bullfight. The arena was cleared as the ships obeyed orders and sheered away. One destroyer trained her searchlights on the wreck— long, long pencils of intense white light reaching for miles through the darkness—and the *Jamaica* came in like a matador for the kill. She swung round and a salvo of torpedoes leaped from her deck and began their fifty-mile-an-hour run toward the target. At that very moment a great billow of smoke eddied out from the *Scharnhorst*'s sides and hid her, but the *Jamaica* put her helm over and sent another salvo of torpedoes hurrying after the first.

With the tremendous explosions when they hit the mark, the smoke cleared away, and the *Scharnhorst* was revealed for the last time, on her side, with her bottom exposed, and yet with the flames of her ammunition fires still spouting from her. Then the smoke closed around her again and she went to the bottom, while the British cruisers raced in to try to pick up survivors. There is on record the comment made by one of the British sailors who went into that smoke, but it is not well to repeat it. More than one thousand men had burnt in those flames.

It is hard to criticize the Nazi tactics or the Nazi strategy. The *Scharnhorst* came out and was destroyed, yet if she had stayed at home the naval historian of the future would have condemned the Nazi High Command for her inactivity. She refused to face Burnett's wildcat attack at the opening of the day, although we know now that nothing worse could have happened to her than actually did happen, and she hardly could have inflicted less damage than she actually did inflict. If she had fought Burnett she might have been disabled and sent to the bottom, leaving us to comment that a more cautious commander would have withdrawn as soon as he was discovered and got clean away.

Yet in the months to come, the Nazi sailor who is ordered out will remember the *Spee* and the *Bismarck* and the *Scharnhorst*, and will go with a reluctance that will not increase his efficiency. And the Japanese, on the other side of the world, must have heard of the loss of the *Scharnhorst* with dismay, for it meant that at least one more British battleship was freed to make the voyage east and add to the pressure of sea power that will slowly constrict Japan to her death.

★   I HAVE NOT YET BEGUN TO FIGHT.

★

                                             —JOHN PAUL JONES

★

GIVE US THIS DAY

SERGEANT SIDNEY STEWART
(WITH JOE WHEELER)

When this book was published by W. W. Norton in 1957, a *New York Times* reviewer labeled it "*The Andersonville* of World War II." The firsthand account of the famous Bataan Death March is so graphic that the *New York Times* reviewer wrote, "There are experiences so terrifying that the act of recording them must involve a journey back into a nightmare world." And the *Times* reviewer summed it up with these words: "Powerful and moving. . . . The Bataan Death March has never been more graphically described in print." The story of Sidney Stewart's imprisonment by the Japanese in World War II is graphic indeed. The book was featured by both the Catholic Digest Book Club and the Lutheran Book Club.

★ ★ ★

Never can I forget a visitor our family had in Panama at the end of

World War II. This missionary educator regaled us with hour after hour of stories having to do with what he and his family had endured at the hands of the Japanese in the Philippines.

One story I'll never forget. Manila was under siege, and food and water were almost impossible to secure at any price. The missionary remembered how he and so many others huddled behind a wall, waiting for the end. One young millionaire, dying of thirst, offered a million dollars to the man who would risk his life by rushing out from behind the wall and scooping up a small can's worth of filthy water in a ditch. There were no takers, for money meant nothing to men and women dying of thirst. The missionary also told us stories retold to him by survivors of the already infamous Bataan Death March.

★ ★ ★

Sidney Stewart begins his story in Manila, only hours after the Japanese shocked the world by bombing Pearl Harbor. High above him and fellow American soldiers, Japanese planes circled like hawks searching for prey.

And suddenly . . . bombs began to fall. But they didn't take them seriously:

We are Americans, I thought, *proud and sure and free.* We had nothing but contempt for the stupid fools blackening the sky. The Japanese must be crazy to attack a city held by Americans.

"I'll bet this war won't last three weeks," Rasmussen said beside me.

I wondered if it would last even one.

Oh it all happened so quickly. On December 14, glaring newspaper headlines trumpeted the sobering news that eighty Japanese transports had landed at Lingayen and forty more at Lamon Bay.

"The Japanese were on the island. Slowly it became clear that we were nearly helpless, that our equipment was old, and that most of our planes had been destroyed on the ground the day the war started. . . . Now the radios urged the people to have faith. Help was on the way from the States."

But help was *not* on the way.

On Christmas Eve, the order came to evacuate Manila.

Next day, as they rode through the city, they passed group after group of Filipinos who looked on with disbelief. "We had always been the dominant, unconquerable Americans, almost like gods. But now we were running and leaving them to their fate."

Just before Sergeant Stewart's group was to leave the doomed city, he remembered later, "Suddenly I felt a presence in the room. It was a rather small man, dressed in the white tropical habit of a priest. He didn't say a word, but in his sad eyes I felt a strength. . . . His kind, thin face was tanned and softly crossed with lines that indicated a quickness to smile or to deepen with sympathy. I thought he had the kindest smile I had ever seen." His name: Father Bill Cummings.

Later on, Stewart and Cummings boarded a barge, and once away from the pier, they silently looked back at the great city, now an inferno. Suddenly they heard the roar of planes above. And they had no protection. "Then I felt someone put his hand on my arm."

"'Don't be afraid, son.' Don't be afraid! I turned and looked into Father Cummings's eyes. They were calm and he smiled. 'You know, son, the two strongest forces in mankind, the two strongest forces on earth, are fear and love. You might call love, faith. The two forces cannot exist side by side. If you have enough faith, you will have no fear!'"

Shortly afterwards, Stewart and his company disembarked onto the shore of the Bataan peninsula, and the chaplain returned with the barge to burning Manila. The army now marched northward to battle the Japanese. Soon the shelling began on the defenseless marchers, for the sky was owned by Japanese planes.

Day followed nightmarish day, and vainly the soldiers searched the skies for American planes that never came. No one ever thought of surrendering, for it was known the Japanese took no prisoners.

Stewart could hear, in the midst of the incessant bombing, a man in a nearby foxhole, praying, "Oh God, don't let me die. Take care of me. Don't let me die, God. Please, God, don't let me die."

"At last we received no more food at all. The fury of the fighting made it impossible to deliver what rations we might have had. Our front line was pushed back and back by the Japanese onslaught, gradually crowding us toward the sea. Malaria and dengue fever, diarrhea, hunger and weariness tore at our ranks. The unrelenting sun was like an open furnace glaring in the sky, and the unburied dead lay bloating and yellow over the battle ground.

Communications were gone. Our artillery was almost on the infantry line. We began to admit openly that help from the States might not reach us in time. Ammunition was running short. We had plenty of big ammunition, but we had lost all of our larger artillery to the Japanese. Every ounce of the smaller stuff was precious now. Each shot had to count.

At night the jungle became a horrible thing. The huge artillery shells guttered their way through the sky and then burst into man-made daylight. Also, we were frightened by smaller things. The Jap planes dropped packages of firecrackers behind our lines. They exploded like ripping machine-gun fire. They made us feel we were surrounded. We were tired, exhausted, and the days were long. Could we hold out?

The end came on April 8th, 1942. One of the men from a nearby Company rushed to us.

'It's happened!' he yelled hysterically. 'The Fifty-First has given way. Their lines are broken. They're running for their lives, and the Twenty-Sixth has given way on the other side. What'll we do? Where'll we go?'

We sat stunned. The worst is never truly expected, regardless of how long the mind is gauged for it. Hope throws up a blind wall that cuts off the most skilled imagination. . . . Our last officer had been killed that morning and we had nowhere to turn for authority or direction. Every sergeant held his men together through each man's frightened desire to be told what to do. Men hoped to keep their minds a blank against terrifying reality. The indecision broke like a river dam, and everyone began talking and yelling at once.

I sat there paralyzed. Weldon jumped up and yelled to the other men. Then he worked his way to each one of the foxholes telling them the news. We waited, speechless and stunned, until he crawled back into the foxhole with us.

'They're all game to try to make it to Corregidor' he said grimly. 'So we'd better start.'

Somehow, like sleepless zombies, we started making our way back through the jungle. No man spoke of the thoughts that were in his mind. We moved slowly, certain that movement, any movement, was better than sitting still waiting for it to come. So we moved back, making our way through the jungle.

Darkness fell quickly in the jungle. The night was lit with a million flares that burst in the sky above us. The earth began to shake and reverberate as the ammunition dumps exploded. It was a nightmare in hell. The end of the world had come. I reached forward and gripped Rass's arm, wanting to feel the reality of someone near me. As the ammunition dumps went, the stark trees shook and danced to the roaring blasts. You could read a book by the lurid glare of the constant explosions. The artillery pounded away and shell fragments screamed through the air. The demolition of unused airplane bombs vomited diabolic destruction, shaking the ground like an earthquake.

We went on through the jungle and down the mountainside like frightened, lost children. I felt as if I were hiding beneath an iron tub and giants were beating the sides with huge stone mallets.

With each blow the sparks cast themselves down upon me, searing into my brain.

We came to a little clearing on the hillside. The men threw themselves down and rested without speaking. No one dared to speak for fear of letting loose a chain of emotions within himself. Each man sensed the fear within his companions. We had a horrible feeling of loss and loneliness. Loneliness, for death we knew was coming. And death strikes each man as an individual. You are alone, no matter how many are there.

We lay still, watching the flares and feeling the trembling of the ground beneath us.

'All right, you guys.' I heard Weldon's gruff voice. 'We're not going to lie here all night. We gotta get going.'

'Going where?' someone said. 'We might as well stay here and face it.'

'Aw, shut up!' someone else snarled. 'You don't know what's going to happen.'

I understood for a moment that strong rationalization in every man's mind. With the inevitable right upon us, some were refusing to accept it.

We crawled slowly to our feet. Staggering, we started back through the jungle and down the mountainside until we reached a road. In the flares the white coral road was like a white ribbon that stretched down to the beach.

Ahead of us we could see the city of Marivales and the native grass shacks, aburst with flame like giant torches. Their flames danced like mad sprites against the darkness of the sea behind. By now we were surrounded by thousands of other men. Their faces showed wide eyes and mouths tight with fear. None of them knew where he was going, but cattle-like followed the man ahead.

We wandered down to the beach. Waiting, hoping against hope, waiting. Still the planes crashed their bombs from overhead and the artillery gutted among us. The men no longer sought protection. As the pieces of shrapnel screamed by our ears there was something almost comforting about the sound. Wouldn't it be better to die now than to face what we were sure awaited us?

'Tell everyone to get rid of their souvenirs!' someone passed the word. 'Get rid of everything you have that the Japanese might suspect belonged to their troops.'

Stupidly, I wondered why. We gathered what was left of our Company and built a little fire on the beach and the Company records were burned. Then each man came forward and emptied his papers upon it.

It was a small fire, an insignificant speck against the giant flares and the burning city below us. How small, but how important it was. As its flames danced, it reduced to ashes all records of what we were and who we were. Then the Company flag was brought forward and laid on the fire and I turned my face and looked back toward the jungle. I could not stand to see those colors burning. Suddenly I heard Weldon crying beside me, and the sobs shook his body.

'The Americans didn't even try to send us help,' he choked. 'They deserted us.'

I turned to comfort him but he didn't need me. Hughes, always the weakest of our party, the most easily frightened, stood there holding his arm, patting his back, encouraging him. Then I saw two men carry forward the American flag. They opened it and shook it out in the wind.

In the flares, the bright red-and-white stripes and the little stars in the blue background danced for a moment. Soon it would be a memory of what we stood for. They let one corner of the flag touch the little fire. The flames licked up through the red and white stripes toward the blue. I noticed that all the men were crying, and I could feel the tears as they fell on my cheeks. I gritted my teeth, almost hating America. Hating America who had left us here.

'We fought all this time, thinking that America would send us help,' John said.

It was hard for me to watch him cry. He complained so seldom. I knew what the burning of that flag meant to him and to the men standing around me.

When the last sparkle of it had been reduced to white ashes, we lay down exhausted on the sand of the beach and waited for the morning light, but we did not sleep. Each man stared silently at the sky, clutching his own thoughts, examining his own soul, waiting for what the sun and the day and the Japanese Army would bring.

The order to destroy our guns was passed among us, no man knowing whence it came. We set about the procedure as we had been taught.

'This old thing ain't never been any good,' Weldon said slowly, running his fingers over the stock of the old Enfield rifle like a mother caressing a child. 'Be plain sabotage to let some Nip have an ornery gun like you.'

John kept staring at the smoke rising from the ruins of Marivales, only his eyes alive in the white delicate face. 'Even now the devastation has begun, and half the business of destruction done,' he quoted from Goldsmith's *Deserted Village,* as though he stood all alone searching for beauty in a world falling apart before his eyes, a world that bewildered him. Tears came into my eyes and I wiped them on my dirty sleeve.

Rass laid his hand on my arm. I hadn't realized till then how I was trembling. His face was drawn and tired, but his eyes were dry and he tried desperately to smile.

'Don't think they'll let us surrender.' His lips trembled and he looked away, then back. 'Never did get to tell you about a horse I had once.'

I didn't listen. The flares no longer brightened in the morning light, but their smoke snaked through the sky. The dust from the road just above me was thick, and mingled with the fumes like white powder. As I looked at the faces of the men I felt a tight binding within me. I jerked my eyes away and looked back to the mountains. Mount Bataan with its cool crater stretched away into the high blue sky. It was unperturbed, untouched by the tiny men who crawled like ants over its sides. Soon I saw strange tanks rumbling down the road, the dust rising beside them like smoke.

Japanese soldiers were coming out of the brush. They walked to the edge of the road and stood looking down at us. I expected at any moment to feel machine-gun bullets ripping through my flesh. The tanks stopped and the turrets were opened. I saw one Japanese officer raise himself up. He stood on the inside of the tank, looking over the turret at the bedraggled, heartbroken army. A smile lit his lips, a smile of triumph. Then he screamed orders to the Japanese soldiers.

'They want us to move up on to the road,' said a voice. 'They want us all to come up and bring all of our stuff.'

We struggled to our feet.

'Let's all stick together,' Rass suggested. 'Whatever happens, it'll be easier to take it that way.'

We started walking toward the road, not knowing what was to happen.

★ ★ ★

We reached the road and the Japanese motioned haughtily for us to stand in the depressions along the sides of the old coral highway. Holding their rifles flat and ready, they moved among us, slowly, cooly suspicious, their eyes glaring.

With the gasping breath of relief the word was passed along. 'They're going to make us prisoners.' Suddenly the deafening roar of the explosions stopped. All firing ceased.

The quick silence was an odd sound to our ears, so used to the war. An occasional rifle shot cracked in the distance, ringing with a hollow echo over the jungle. When I looked at the dust-covered faces of our captors, I felt the cold hatred in their eyes, and wondered how we would be treated. We laid our stuff out on the ground in front of us and unrolled our packs. Most of us had very little, as a soldier throws everything away but the very essential.

The Japanese officers walked back and forth in the road, their samurai swords clacking against their black boots. By contrast the Jap enlisted men were dressed in patched and ragged uniforms and wrapped to the knees in puttees like those the American soldiers had worn in the First World War. An order was screamed in Japanese. I don't know why we all looked at John, expecting him to translate for us. But of course he couldn't. The Japs began knocking our helmets off with the tips of their bayonets. They fell to the ground with the clamor of tin wash pans.

'Just look at these poor guys,' Rass whispered. I looked around at the Filipinos and the Americans lined up in the road. Their faces were half-starved and dirty from the swirling chalky dust of the coral road glaring in the sun. Their clothes were rags and there was fear and hatred in their tired, red eyes. They were expecting something very bad, and now it was coming.

The Japanese soldiers began to lose restraint. They jerked off watches and fountain pens. Then they lost their tempers, slugging and beating the men up and down the line. A boy who stood near me cried out with pain as one of the Jap guards smashed a fist into his face. The guard laughed, then raised the butt of his rifle, crashing it down over the boy's head. Groaning, the kid sagged to his knees. With all his strength the guard swung the butt again and the boy's head made a dull, splattering sound as it split open before our eyes.

The body convulsed, shuddering, and the fingers grabbed the ground. Then it lay still. One of the Jap soldiers laughed and kicked the dead American with the toe of his shoe. I hated them with a violent hatred.

We started out on the road, leaving our little handful of possessions behind us. Every few yards more Japanese materialized from the bushes around us. We were covered by the white dust stirred up by the horse-drawn artillery and the trucks. Jap soldiers, as they filed along, would jerk an American out of line and beat him, then shove him back into the line. There was no reason in the performance. They did it purely for entertainment.

Before we had gone two miles our shirts were stripped from our bodies. The sun reached straight above us, beating down on our bare heads. My head began to ache in the blistering heat. My eyes seemed to bulge from my head. I wanted water more than anything. We kept walking and the heat seemed to search out all the strength in me.

'Oh, God, where are we going? Where are we going?' Hughes whimpered. John gave him a savage 'Sshh!'

The afternoon wore on and the Japanese soldiers lining the road became more ferocious. The sun beat on my head and it ached almost to splitting with the heat of it. My skin felt pierced by a million needles of fire. I passed a man lying in the road with his head smashed in, and then another, writhing in misery, clutching his belly in bloody hands. A bayonet had been driven through his intestines. Soon it became commonplace and I saw scores and finally hundreds like them. I began to think only of lifting my feet one at a time and putting them down.

Slowly the darkness fell. The coolness of night descended. I watched men fall to the ground. The Japanese rushed in among us, kicking them with their heavy boots and jabbing them with their bayonets. If the men could not rise they were beaten to death. My hatred gave me strength.

We walked all night and when the dawn came it brought the

sun again. The temperature rose slowly as the sun climbed in the sky. The noon hour came and the midday heat was blistering, searing our skins. But we straggled on, afraid to fall by the side. The heat and the choking dust filled our noses, tearing at our raw throats.

Hughes kept stumbling and whimpering. He walked bent almost in half and the white coral dust covering his hair gave him the appearance of a very old man. John, who never complained, began a rasping cough and his dirt mask was criss-crossed with lines of running sweat.

During the afternoon we came to a cool mountain stream and the Japanese yelled for us to stop. We stood there, knowing we were to get water. The dampness of the ground smelled mossy and wonderful. Looking down at the cool stream bubbling and gurgling over the rocks, I licked my cracked and gritty lips. It looked so clear, so cool, so delicious. If only I could throw myself down into the water and lie there feeling it rush over my body.

We waited and waited, but still they did not allow us to drink. Suddenly one of the men could bear it no longer. He rushed forward, fell on his hands and knees, threw his face into the water. A Japanese non-com ran up, unsheathing his sword and swinging it high.

I heard a quick, ugly swish. Before I could realize what had happened, I saw the head roll away in the stream. The blood and water mingled together, a violent red. The body was stationary for a moment and suddenly the blood gushed out of the gaping hole at the neck like a waterfall. The body lunged forward in the streambed, the hands opening and closing. Feeling sick, I thought, *It is like a chicken with its neck wrung.* I hated myself for the thought. I closed my eyes and gritted my teeth.

The guards yelled for us to go on. They were not going to let us have water. Without stopping or turning we headed up the dusty road glaring in the tropical sun.

'I don't think I can make it much farther,' I heard Hughes whisper. 'I don't feel like I can make it another block.'

'I don't think I can either,' Rass gasped. But then a mile passed.

'Just keep thinking that you're gonna get water up ahead,' Weldon begged, the strength almost gone from his deep voice.

I began to fasten my mind on the thought of water, how good it would taste. My mouth was terribly dry and my tongue felt rough and swollen in my mouth. The dust tasted gritty on my cracked lips. I licked my tongue across them, thinking of water and its taste. Somehow the night passed and the morning sun came again. I remembered passing through Orion and then Pilar.

The sun beat down on my throbbing head. I thought only of bringing my feet up, putting them down, bringing them up. Along the road the jungle was a misty green haze, swimming before my sweat-filled eyes.

The hours dragged by, and a great many of the prisoners reached the end of their endurance. The drop-outs became more numerous. They fell by the hundreds in the road. Some made an effort to rise. Groaning and weeping, they tried to get to their feet. Some succeeded, others fell back helplessly. I wondered that the Jap guards paid no attention. Why? Why did they leave them, when they had killed them before?

Suddenly I knew. There was the crack of a pistol and the shot rang out across the jungle. There was another shot, and more shots, and I knew that, straggling along behind us, was a clean-up squad of Japanese, killing their helpless victims on the white dusty road. The shots rang out through the night, making orange flashes in the darkness. I wondered how soon our bodies would be with the rest. The shots continued, goading us on. I gritted my teeth. 'Oh, God, I've got to keep going. I can't stop. I can't die like that.'

When morning came, John said, 'I can't make it this day. I cannot make it.'

'I can't either, John.'

But we kept on and the sun climbed slowly higher and higher. We passed thousands of American and Filipino bodies bloating and rotting in the sun.

At noon they stopped us. Thee was a flurry of activity up ahead. There were carabao holes beside the road, like pig wallows, with greenish water and slimy scum covering the top. Small gnats and flies buzzed around them. Even so, it was water.

We looked, asking the question with our eyes of our Jap guards. Surprisingly, they nodded, and we ran for it. Falling on our knees, we pushed the scum back from the top of the water with our hands. The stenching liquid was water. When we started down the road again, somehow I felt better.

The murders went on. Death was always at our heels. We struggled to keep going. Weldon pushed Hughes with his shoulder, trying to keep him from falling. Rass half-carried John at times. Then he would shift him to me. We would change positions and I would walk in front with John's hands on my shoulders, holding him up.

On the fifth day we arrived at Orani. They herded us on to the cement patio of an old Spanish church. They motioned for us to sit down, but we were so crowded that we had to sit with our knees hunched up in front of us. After a little while huge caldrons of steaming rice were brought forward and a small handful was ladled out to each one of us. We ate ravenously. But no sooner had we finished eating than the guards ran in among us, screaming, kicking us with their boots, making us get to our feet.

The rest had cramped my muscles and my legs jerked with the effort as we started up the road. Gradually I began to lose consciousness. I was surrounded by a scorching, thirsty haze. My eyes grew dim and I thought only of keeping my feet moving. I had to keep going. Walking, walking. I no longer noticed when the men in my Company fell out. No longer counted the bodies in the road.

Sometime late in the night we started through the outskirts of the Filipino city of Lubao. It may have been a day later, for Weldon told me we had been walking for eight days. In Lubao the Filipinos stood at the open windows of their homes and threw food to us. A scramble started among the prisoners. I watched them through a haze, wondering how they had the strength to fight. The guards screamed in frenzy, stamping and grinding the food under their feet, and beating a man if he picked up a piece of it.

We were herded on through the streets of the city, much like the other cities, with bamboo homes set on stilts. At the end of one street there was an ancient Alamo-style church. My eyes burned with the sun and sweat and dust, but when I looked at the compassion and pity on the faces of the Filipinos I became more determined. *I will go on*, I thought.

Somehow we reached the other side of the city. They marched us into an open field. An interpreter screamed that we were not to sit down. The nerves in my legs began an uncontrollable jerking and I wondered what we were waiting for. Weldon stood as though propped up by some unseen force, his eyes staring without focus. Hughes leaned against him with his knees sagging. His once-blond hair was muddy with sweat and dust, and his face was drawn and cadaverous. John swayed drunkenly, his hand gripping Rass's shoulder. Rass's bloodshot eyes grew suddenly alive. I followed the look in them.

A guard walked by with an American head stuck on the end of his bayonet. My stomach turned over at the sight. Blood was running from the neck and from the open lips. The teeth were clinched in a ghastly smile and the eyes protruded. I turned my eyes away, but I saw three other Japs, each of them with an American head on a bayonet. They walked in among us and we fell silent, watching them with black, deadly hatred.

Night came at last, yet we continued to stand there. If a man slumped to his knees the guards rushed in, jabbing him with their bayonets or kicking him until he either stood or fell groaning to the ground.

When morning came we started again. The day was like the rest, horribly hot and thirsty. But we walked and the day passed and the night passed.

'We're on the outskirts of San Fernando,' Rass said. His voice sounded like an echo in a cave. 'They'll give us food here. They're going to put us on a train.'

I shook my head. I could not trust myself to speak. I did not believe it. The only thing that gave me hope was the fact that they didn't kill us. They must have some reason for marching us, goading us, beating us on like this. Surely somewhere was the end of this trail of blood and death.

'We've been walking nine days now,' John said. The words rasped from his parched throat.

We went on through the streets of San Fernando. My head was bursting under the constant glare of the sun, and I lost consciousness. When my head cleared again I was on a boxcar.

'I don't know what happened to you. I dragged you that last two miles,' Rass said quietly. 'You kept falling. You were kicked and beaten but you always managed to get back on your feet.'

I looked around. John and Weldon and Hughes were still there. They sat holding their heads in their hands. . . . I looked down. My feet were wet with blood.

On April 21st, twelve days after our surrender, we reached Camp O'Donnell. It was said that more than fourteen thousand men died on the march. The living also were dying men at the end, haunted by fear, eaten by pain and fever.

Sometimes I think we all died on the march. Sometimes I feel sure that all the things that came later were just a fevered dream, and that somewhere back on those blood-soaked miles there is another body. . . ."

★ ★ ★

As the world perceives it, the Bataan Death March was now over, with fourteen of the thirty thousand G.I. prisoners of war now dead. But, according to Stewart, that was only the beginning of a three-year-long nightmare of torture, sickness, and death.

The remaining sixteen thousand were now herded into Camp O'Donnell in Wzon, where men continued to die from starvation, dehydration, and dysentery. Beside each of the shacks were stacks of bodies pulled there by the living, for they had nowhere else to put them. In the hot tropical sun the bodies swelled and bloated until they were no longer recognizable as the bodies of men.

Suddenly, the sergeant heard a familiar voice: it was the chaplain, Father Cunningham! Stewart said to him, "'Father, they say you've become famous all over the world for your statement that there are no atheists in foxholes. They quote it now, they say, in the newspapers all over America.'

He didn't answer me. I don't think he even heard. He kept staring at the silent, hopeless faces of the prisoners around him.

'I must work harder,' he said with a sigh. 'These men need me.'"

That night, as spotlights sprayed across the barbed wire fences, Father Cunningham spoke to the despairing soldiers, "It is a simple thing of faith," he said tenderly. "A thing to believe in, to hold to. . . . And though we should soon die, and be stacked with that pile of bodies ourselves," he said, holding his hand over his mouth to keep out the black flies, "is it not best to have God at our side? It is a lonely thing to die alone, feeling no presence beside you, feeling that no one cares. If you have faith and you believe, you are never alone. You cannot be lonely, even if you die." He looked up at the sky and was silent for a moment. In his eyes there was a terrible sadness.

The stack of bodies grew, until there were thousands, and flies swarmed by the millions. Vultures dropped down to the stacks, tearing at the flesh and eyes of the bodies. The stench was overpowering. The men grew mean as they weakened, and the stronger became sullen and selfish. Father Cunningham somehow was always where the need was greatest, and favored no one more or less than another.

By the end of May, half of the sixteen thousand that made it to the camp were dead. Finally, the Japanese decided to treat the prisoners better. They were fed enough to enable the survivors to regain some of their strength. Sergeant Stewart and a number of others now set out to learn Japanese so that they could better understand, and perhaps even empathize with, their captors.

Only surviving prisoners of war know how powerful friendships forged in such conditions can be. As Stewart put it, "loyalty to our friends prevented us from trying to escape, and a man needed friends to survive in prison camp. They worked beside him and shared their food when he was sick. They bathed him when he was burning up with fever. They talked to him when his spirits were low and sometimes saved his life. His friends would die if he escaped."

★ ★ ★

Years passed. . . . One Sunday in the fall of 1944, for the first time in over three years, the prisoners were distributed cards and told that each man could write a ten-word message to a loved one, and that the cards would be mailed.

No small thanks to Father Cummings, Sergeant Stewart and others began to lose their hatred of the Japanese. One of the prisoners put it this way, "most of us now speak their language and we have learned to understand their superstitions, their beliefs, their religion, their way of life. Many of them are like men all over the world, no better, no worse. They too like to take out their photographs and show pictures of their wives and children. They too long for the war to end so they can go home again."

One memorable day, the prisoners heard a different sound in the sky: an American war plane—then another—and another. But the prisoners' euphoria proved premature for some of their most terrible days were now ahead of them.

The prisoners were herded back to Manila, and into the foul holds of ships. Stewart's group, consisting of over six hundred, packed into an area large enough for only a hundred. And the ceiling was only five feet high. The hold became hotter and hotter, until it became a veritable inferno. Prisoners began to scream, crying for air and begging for water. Some men went insane. Some laughed hysterically. Some tore at each other, fighting and pushing. Some men became beasts, cutting the throats of others in order to drink their blood. A son went insane and proceeded to kill his father. Some resorted to drinking their own urine for they were perishing of thirst—and then they retched and retched.

"Suddenly from the depths of the hold I heard a voice like the voice of God. Father Cummings began to speak. The sound was clear and resonant and made me feel he was talking to me alone. The men became quiet.

'Our Father who art in heaven, hallowed be Thy name. Thy kingdom come. Thy will be done on earth as it is in heaven. . . .' The voice went on.

'Have faith,' he continued. 'Believe in yourselves and in the goodness of one another. Know that in yourselves and in those that stand near you, you see the image of God. For mankind is in the image of God.'"

Shortly afterwards, American planes attacked the convoy. Explosions were heard in different parts of the ship. Fires broke out, and the heat became unbearable. Knowing they were dead men if they remained where they were, the prisoners, weak as they were, desperately clawed their way onto the top deck and battled the Japanese. Then a new wave of allied planes came in and began strafing the deck. The prisoners, whether they could swim or not, shed what rags they still wore, and jumped overboard. Now they were strafed and bombed by the planes and machine-gunned from the ships. The sea turned red from the carnage.

Those who made it ashore were eventually permitted to climb out without being shot. Twelve hundred were all who now remained alive of the thirty thousand. Most of the men now being naked, the sun scorched them, and their bodies screamed out their need of water. At night, men would get the chills. Diarrhea attacked with a vengeance, and more and more men died every night. Eventually, the starving men were brought just enough uncooked rice to keep them alive.

Next day, they were told to move again, and any who could not walk were clubbed to death by the Japanese. But even here, Father Cummings kept faith alive. Yet, "he was very thin and less strong than the rest of us, with a skinny, naked little body and scanty, white hair."

Once again, they were herded into barges. The water they were given to drink was half ocean water—yet they had to drink it in order to survive.

By January of 1945, Stewart observed, "Misery had made us all alike. We were no longer men, save in brief flashes. Merely hulks of human flesh which contained only a desire to eat, a desire for water, and a hope and prayer to live." More men were dying every hour. The stench of the bodies in the hold became so great that it was spreading to the upper part of the ship. Finally, the guards threw ropes down into the hold and commanded us to tie the bodies together. They called some of the men on deck and allowed the bodies to be hauled up. Then the bodies were splashed into the water with weights to pull them to the bottom of the sea.

Each day, as the ship moved father north, it grew colder, and now the naked men huddled together trying to keep each other warm. Finally, they approached Taiwan.

Early the following morning, American planes attacked again. Bombs fell. The ship became an inferno, and walls and decks collapsed on the prisoners. Stewart was now paralyzed from the waist down—it was assumed his back was broken. Nearly three hundred of the prisoners died in the attack.

"Then, very low, I heard Father Cummings praying—praying to the God he believed in and that he wanted us to have faith in. I wanted to pray, but I couldn't."

That terrible day passed, and another, and another—without either food or water. The Japanese turned a cold shoulder on their anguish, muttering, "They were your planes that bombed us. We don't care if you die. They killed our men too."

"I heard an almost hysterical weeping. Some were giving up hope. Then I heard Father Cummings, 'Listen to me, men! You must listen to me!' The crying stopped and there was no more groaning. Then in his deep, clear resonant voice he began to pray. It was the Lord's Prayer. It floated like a benediction through the hold, caressing every one of us.

'Our Father who art in Heaven, hallowed be Thy name. Thy kingdom come. Thy will be done on earth as it is in Heaven. . . .' I felt that God listened, that God watched us, and that God cared."

Once again, bodies stacked up. Again slings were lowered and the corpses were stacked on little rafts in groups of about twenty-five each. Stewart noted, "These men, the living, were almost as much a part of the dead as the bodies. They went about their work in a dazed, helpless way, lifting the bodies of their best friends, moving and separating the wounded from those who were dead." They took the bodies—all four hundred of them—ashore and burned them.

Now they were greeted with the news that those pitifully few who yet lived were to be taken to Japan! Stewart was carried aboard yet another ship.

The cold increased, and there was no water to drink. "In the evening, as it grew dark in the hold, Father Cummings stood and prayed. He started with the Lord's Prayer, and then said a prayer for the day, and for those who had died, and those who were dying around us.

It grew colder and colder, and some snow and sleet began to fall down in the open hatch. We felt ourselves freezing. Our teeth chattered all the time. We were emaciated, almost bloodless, and the cold was unbearable." Some men became demented. Of the nineteen priest/chaplains who had left Manila, only Father Cummings yet lived.

Sergeant Stewart looked forward every hour for night to come, when Father Cummings stood and said his prayer again. "I lived only for that prayer of faith and hope. It was the only strength I had. His voice was like the voice of God to me. I knew that Rass felt the same. Rass, who was always so much more religious than I. He was now so weak that it was all he could do to stand. Yet I knew he too lived for that prayer in the evening.

Men were dying at the rate of twenty and thirty a day. Every morning their bodies were wrapped with rope, drawn up through the hold, and dropped into the sea.

Now Father Cummings began to weaken. He had been passing blood many days with dysentery. He was so weak that he could not walk. His lips were parched and cracked and his hands moved convulsively up and down his throat. I knew that he couldn't make it much longer. I prayed silently to myself that I would die before he did, so I would not have to see him die.

But that evening, as it was growing dark down in the hold, and the faint light that came through the hatch was nearly gone, Father Cummings begged me, 'Can you lift your arm behind me? I can't stand, but my voice will carry. They will hear my prayer.'

I pushed my shoulder in behind him and put my arms around him and held him up. Faltering, he began to speak.

'Men! Men, can you hear my voice?'

Slowly he began to pray. 'Our Father . . . hallowed be Thy name. . . .' The cries of the men became still. I concentrated on the voice that soothed me and gave me strength and the will to live. Then I felt his body shiver and tremble in my arms. He gasped for air and there was a terrible pain written on his face. He gritted his teeth, sighed, and went on.

'Thy will . . . in Heaven.'

I felt him tremble again as if he wanted to cough. His hands fluttered and his eyelids almost closed. Then with superhuman effort he spoke again.

'Give us this day . . .'

I felt his body go tense all over. He relaxed and his hand fell by his side. I waited, but his eyes looked straight ahead. The eyelids no longer flickered. I knew he was dead, but I continued to hold him.

Rass crawled beside me. He lifted Father Cummings's hand and felt for his pulse. 'Lay him down, Sid,' he said evenly. 'He's gone. . . . He's gone now.'

I cradled his head against my shoulder. I didn't want to lay him down. I couldn't bear to face the fact that he was gone.

Rass reached across the body and gripped my arm. 'Sid, he died like he would have wanted to die, praying to the God that he believed in, to the God that gave him strength.'

'Why did he have to die, Rass? Why did he have to leave us?'

'Don't think about the fact that he's gone. Try to think of his last words. The last thing he tried to give us.'

Rass went on calmly. 'You know his last words were, 'Give us this day.' We must try only to live until we can see the sun in the morning, you and I, and we'll make it. Live only for one day, for just twenty-four more hours.'"

Next morning, as the first rays of dawn came into the hold, the ropes were lowered into the hold once again. Among the other bodies was now that of Father Cummings. "Slowly the body started to rise as though it was floating out of the hold. When the sun struck Father Cummings's body, it seemed to reflect a golden light. I watched that golden light and the body as it floated higher and higher into the air." And then it was over.

★ ★ ★

They finally reached Japan. Many disembarked like Sergeant Stewart, on hands and knees. "Snow and sleet were falling, and the ground was wet and slushy. Feebly I pulled myself, and my teeth began an uncontrollable chattering. My hands and arms were blue with the cold. I had never been so cold in all my life." The other men too—all naked and still—were bitterly cold. Their bodies were blue and their lips purple. A man would drop into a coma by the road. "We went nearly three blocks. The blocks were like a hundred miles." Finally they crawled into an old, empty warehouse. Three hundred, maybe less, out of thirty thousand.

Yet, as days passed, more and more died. No medicine, no additional attention of any kind. Some days, no food at all. "Occasionally when we cried out for food, they brought in buckets of their leavings, their slop, and dumped that in the middle of the floor. We crawled forward, eating from the floor with our hands."

The days dragged into weeks. More men died. Every morning the Japanese came into the room. If a prisoner was in a coma they caught him by the feet and pulled him across the floor and outdoors into the snow. Then they stacked him with the other bodies waiting for burial.

Each day, Rass and Stewart kept each other alive. But one day, Rass too was gone. "All at once I knew that God had taken Rass home. God was good."

★ ★ ★

With the death of his last buddy, the Sergeant just let go, losing all track of time and place. Dimly he was aware that he yet lived; why, he did not know. Always, it seemed, he was being moved: moved to Korea, and then moved again to far off Manchuria.

In time, he regained awareness and looked up at faces he'd never seen before. He wondered why anyone had bothered to keep transporting his wreck of a body from place to place to place, for no one knew any more who he was.

He wondered again and again why he yet lived, when so many thousands did not. Why anyone had bothered to keep a cripple alive. Why had God permitted him alone of all his friends to survive? It would be much later before he would understand: in order to write one of the most deeply moving and redemptive war stories ever written.

Finally, liberation came out of the turrets of Russian tanks. And Sidney Stewart, because of his precarious physical condition, was one of the first to be carried aboard an American plane.

The propellers began to spin: He was going home.

But the words—the words returned to him again, again, and yet again:

"Our Father who art in Heaven. . . .

Give us this day. . . ."

★ ★ ★

Sidney Stewart was a member of the infamous Bataan Death March after the fall of the Philippines. He wrote during the second half of the twentieth century.

★
★
★

DUTY IS THE SUBLIMEST
WORD IN THE ENGLISH
LANGUAGE. DO YOUR DUTY IN
ALL THINGS. YOU CANNOT DO
MORE. YOU SHOULD NEVER
WISH TO DO LESS.

—ROBERT E. LEE

DOOLITTLE'S RAID ON TOKYO

MARTIN CAIDIN

P earl Harbor was, in the words of FDR, "a day that will live in infamy." But that term also applied to the criminal negligence of the American South Pacific military leadership in Hawaii. Because of this, our ships, planes, and men were just so many sitting ducks to the pilots of the Japanese Zeros.

Morale on America's mainland plunged. Would the mainland be next? With our fleet disabled or sunk, who would protect us?

What was needed—desperately needed—was something to cheer about. Enter Lt. Col. Doolittle.

★ ★ ★

The flight deck on the aircraft carrier *Hornet* came alive with running men. At the aft deck Navy crews crisscrossed sixteen twin-engine bombers so tightly together the tail assemblies of the planes jutted out over the water.

Long rows of bombs on low-slung lorries rolled across the deck, and into each of the sixteen planes went four five-hundred-pounders. Even as the missiles were secured in the bays Navy deck crews rocked the planes back and forth, trying to break any big air bubbles which might have formed in the gas tanks—so that a few more precious quarts could be squeezed in.

Plunging ahead as fast as her screws could move her the big carrier charged into giant waves, dipping and rising crazily. Water continually broke the high bow and sent green spray cascading through the air. It was forbidding weather for a carrier take-off, especially with sixteen big bombers which had never been designed for the sea, and which had never before taken-off from a carrier deck! But this was the Big Gamble, the first attempt to raid the Japanese homeland, and necessity outweighed the appalling risks.

Then it was time. With Lieutenant Colonel James H. Doolittle at the controls, the lead plane was pulled to the starting line. Soon the props began to turn and the engines spat blue-white smoke as Doolittle revved up for take-off.

Everyone watched the Navy man at the port bow. He lifted a checkered flag, swung it faster and faster in a circle—the signal for Doolittle to open his engines wide. The Navy man waited, timing every move carefully. Another signal, and the crewmen yanked free the chocks beneath the bomber's wheels. Finally the flag went up, snapped forward, and Doolittle's B-25 started rolling down the 467 feet of deck—all the room he had.

It was timed perfectly. The deck pitched upward just as the bomber started to lift. Flaps down at full, motors wide open, Doolittle's bomber plunged into the teeth of the howling gale.

Then the next plane was in line, waiting, finally thundering into the wind. And the next, and the next, until all sixteen bombers were gone. One by one they raced away toward the west, toward the home islands of Japan. Single file—hit and run.

This was April 18, 1942—the date set for the first attack against the "sacred soil" of Nippon. The first blow struck back by Americans since the devastating defeat at Pearl Harbor on December 7, 1941.

We had been at war with Japan for four and a half months. In virtually every battle the Japanese had soundly whipped us. They enjoyed absolute control of the air. Their fleet ruled the seas. The gallant defenders of Wake Island had been swamped. Guam was lost. On April 9 the exhausted and beaten defenders of Bataan laid down their arms to victorious Japanese troops. Pearl Harbor still held the bodies of hundreds of men trapped in sunken ships. Islands fell one after the other, and Australia itself was threatened with invasion.

Despair, defeat and humiliation. These were the conditions which faced the American people. National morale was at its lowest ebb.

But before April 18 passed into history the entire country rejoiced with sensational news. American planes had bombed Japan! We had struck back! It mattered not at all that the raid was a token blow. It was enough that we had started to erase the shame of almost continuous defeat at the hands of a people we had long held in scorn.

The plan to bomb the Japanese homeland was conceived originally during the dark days of January 1942. There was a desperate need to stimulate the morale of our people. Army and Navy strategists came up with an idea: Why not strike directly at the heart of Japan?

The daring scheme was fraught throughout with peril. It called for the launching of Army medium bombers from an aircraft carrier which would transport the planes to a point close enough to Japan for the planes to reach their targets and fly onward.

These planes would strike out the twelve hundred miles across the East China Sea to bases in eastern China. Fuel supplies would await them, and they would then proceed to Chung-king, to be based permanently in the Far East under command of General Stillwell.

General H. H. Arnold personally selected Lieutenant Colonel

James H. Doolittle to lead the bombing strike. The colonel picked his twenty-four crews from the ranks of the 34th, 89th, and 95th Squadrons of the 17th Bombardment Group, then assigned to the 8th Air Force. Every man was a volunteer, although none among them had any idea at the time that Japan was their eventual destination.

Doolittle lost no time in going ahead with special training. First the bombers flew to Minneapolis where mechanics cut away the belly turrets and installed new auxiliary fuel tanks in the fuselage; the crews even had fifty gallons in ten tins to pour into the crawl-way tank.

The big question was whether the B-25, loaded with 1,141 gallons of fuel and 2,000 pounds of bombs, could take off from a crowded carrier deck. Had the pilots known what was in store for them they would have cried, "Impossible!" But they were never told until actually aboard the *Hornet* that they would take off from that ship to attack Japan.

With modifications completed the pilots began special training at Eglin Field, Florida. They were told that they would be required to take off under minimum distances, and so were not surprised when Navy officers appeared to coach them in their new skill. For twenty-four days the crews practiced minimum take-off runs, making the B-25s do tricks the designers would never have believed.

By March 24, when orders were received to report to the Alameda Naval Air Station on San Francisco Bay, every pilot had taken off at least twice within a distance of seven hundred to seven hundred fifty feet, with the airplane loaded to thirty-one thousand pounds.

Since the Mitchells would bomb from minimum altitude the men removed the secret Norden bombsights. Captain C. R. Greening came up with a simple, twenty-cent device he called the "Mark Twain" to replace the elaborate optical instrument; it was one of the great improvised weapons of the war.

With their belly guns removed, the bomber crews provided protection against direct rear attacks by installing wooden replicas of fifty-caliber machine guns in the tails.

And still the crews knew only that they were destined for a special mission. They flew long hours at heights with propeller blades skimming the ocean surface. Each plane made repeated runs to its target at zero height, climbing quickly to fifteen hundred feet to drop its bombs, and then racing away at high speed.

Meanwhile, negotiations were under way with Chiang Kai-shek to provide landing flares and fueling facilities at airfields at Kwilin, Kian, Yushan, Chuchow, and Lishui. It is not generally known that Chiang bitterly opposed these arrangements, since the officers of the China-Burma-India Command who discussed our requirements with him gave no specific reason to Chiang of the need for such preparations.

Not until the ships were at sea and the raid committed did the Chinese leader learn the details. Every field but the one at Chuchow was ready on time.

North of Midway Island, *Hornet* and her seven-ship escort rendezvoused with carrier *Enterprise* and the latter's escort of two cruisers, four destroys and an oiler. The sixteen vessels formed Task Force 16, commanded by Vice Admiral William F. Halsey. *Hornet*, helpless with her crowded deck, and her dive bombers below decks stripped of their wings, would have to be protected by planes from *Enterprise*.

As the task force moved toward its destiny off Japan, Doolittle's men reviewed carefully their attack plans. The hoped to be able to reach a point only four hundred and fifty miles off the Japanese coast before take-off. The decision of the Navy to send its precious carriers this close to Japan was a daring one, for there was always the double danger that they might come under attack of Japanese land-based bombers, or that they might be caught by a superior enemy carrier force.

Doolittle estimated that his outside limit of safety was a take-off six hundred and fifty miles from the Japanese coast—any greater distance would court suicide. A premature take-off would endanger the crews even if the attack were successful, for the Chinese were not prepared to receive the bombers before 4 a.m. on April 20. If the planes were forced to take off ahead of schedule, there was no way to warn the Chinese of the decision. Navy task forces at sea maintained a rigid communications blackout.

By April 16 Task Force 16 was committed. The bombers were spotted for take-off on *Hornet's* deck. Doolittle's plane, the lead bomber, faced down 467 feet of open deck, while the fuselage of the last Mitchell hung dangerously over the carrier's stern ramp.

But in the Tokyo headquarters of the brilliant Japanese naval strategist, Admiral Isoroku Yamamoto, Commander-in-Chief, Imperial Combined Fleet, news that something was up in the Pacific had been known for the past six days.

The admiral's intelligence staff had advised him that their interpretations of wireless messages of the American Pacific fleet indicated the probable approach of an enemy carrier task force close to the homeland. They felt that the Americans might launch a carrier plane strike against the main Japanese island of Honshu.

Yamamoto ordered immediate stringent security measures taken. By April 12 every available patrol vessel was cruising the seas to the east within six hundred miles of Japan. Fighter planes moved in from all parts of the country to concentrate about the major cities, with the greatest numbers in the Tokyo area.

Simultaneously, long-range bombers were ordered to fly patrols day and night, and other bombers were held in readiness to strike at the enemy warships when they appeared. If the Americans were to be so foolhardy as to move within range of his bombers, Yamamoto was prepared to deliver the same smashing blows which had sent the dreadnaughts *Prince of Wales* and *Repulse* to the bottom off Malaya in twenty-two minutes, and which had turned the British carrier *Hermes* into a gutted, sinking wreck in fifteen minutes.

There was only one flaw in Yamamoto's defense plans. He did not know that the bombers crowded aboard *Hornet* were long-range, twin-engined B-25s, that they could strike at Japan from several times the maximum distance possible with carrier-based bombers.

And now—during the first hours of April 18—the Japanese and American forces began to meet.

At ten minutes past two the radar observer aboard cruiser *Vincennes* reported a boat not more than ten miles ahead of Task Force 16. Our ships were still seven hundred nautical miles due east of land. The naval officers were astounded—and worried; Japanese patrols were known never to venture this far out to sea! They were unaware, of course, of Yamamoto's countermoves.

Task Force 16 altered course hurriedly to move around the unsuspecting enemy patrol boat. The ships passed unseen in the night, but not until the enemy patrol boat's "blip" had disappeared from the radar screen did the task force officers dare breathe easier.

At the first light of dawn, *Enterprise* launched planes to scout ahead of the fleet. At five o'clock sharp, carrier time, pilots reported a patrol boat forty-two miles ahead of the carriers, and that they in turn must have been seen by the boat's crew.

Whether or not the captain of the patrol vessel went to the trouble of flashing a radio signal will never be known, for the messages were not received in Japan. Tokyo headquarters records show that the first radio flash was received at approximately six-thirty (seven-thirty, carrier time) from Patrol Boat No. 23, the *Nitto-Maru*, on regular duty in the specified danger area.

The boat's captain radioed the visual sighting of several American aircraft carriers approximately six hundred nautical miles east of Inubo Point. Tokyo waited anxiously for a second confirming report, but in vain. Obviously the enemy's planes or warships had destroyed the *Nitto-Maru*.

They were correct. At 0738 hours, carrier time, crewmen

aboard *Hornet* sighted a Japanese patrol boat in the water ahead of the fast-moving carrier. Cruiser *Nashville* and two other warships raced in, sinking the boat with shellfire. But the damage had been done; the warning had been sounded!

The danger now was extreme that the Japanese would attack our carriers. There was no time to waste. At eight o'clock, still ten hours before the planned take-off time, Admiral Halsey ordered the bombers launched at once, or pushed overboard. Doolittle's hopes of a late-afternoon takeoff, a bombing attack in darkness, and arrival over China during daylight, were shattered.

The sighting by the *Nitto-Maru* nearly wrecked the elaborately-planned venture. Doolittle's original estimates of absolute safety called for maximum overwater flight of six hundred and fifty miles. He was at this moment a greater distance from his target. Doolittle offered permission for any man to withdraw from the raid. No one accepted

One of the copilots, Captain Thadd Blanton, reported later: "The extra crew members who were brought along for emergency purposes tried every way they knew to beg, borrow, or steal a seat on the raid. Despite the premature take-off, which practically guaranteed that many of us would die and most of us would crash at the end of the mission, the extra men ran all over the carrier offering a hundred, a hundred and fifty dollars to anyone who would relinquish a spot for them. There were no takers."

Exactly eighteen minutes after Halsey ordered the decks cleared of the B-25s, Doolittle's bomber thundered into the air and headed for Japan. The carrier was exactly six hundred sixty-eight nautical miles from the heart of Tokyo.

And here begins the sequence of events which, because two fateful words were never spoken, enabled Doolittle and his men to survive the elaborate Jap trap.

On the basis of the original radio report received from the

Nitto-Maru, the commander of the Yokosuka Naval Air Station and the Army commander of the Tokyo area issued air raid warnings to their respective units. This alert was received by all installations at 8:30, and fighter planes were held in readiness. They were not, however, to take off until further orders.

The enemy carriers held only single-engine planes; the ships could not possibly be in position to launch their bombers for the attack against Japan for several hours, and the planes would not be over the mainland until late afternoon at the earliest. Or so the Japanese believed.

Exactly at 9:45 a.m. a new battle flash exploded Tokyo headquarters into action. The pilot of a Mitsubishi patrol-bomber flying far off the coast confirmed the presence in the air of enemy planes. The Japanese pilot reported that he had sighted two enemy bombers about five hundred nautical miles east of Tokyo. They were flying low and fast, and headed directly for Tokyo.

Intelligence officers conferred with Admiral Yamamoto. What kind of bombers were seen? The pilot had neglected to say. And since they could only have come from a carrier, they could only be carrier patrols—still beyond striking range of Japan.

The orders stood. Jap fighters would remain on the ground.

This was the moment when the decision was made which was to permit Doolittle and his men to attack Japan. Had that Japanese bomber pilot stated specifically that the planes he saw were "twin-engined"—just two simple words—Yamamoto and his staff would have realized at once the true nature of the impending attack. At the proper moment they would have had fighters in the air to meet Doolittle's raiders; the attackers wouldn't have had a chance. As it was, Naval Headquarters only ordered the standby.

Thus, at twelve noon, when Doolittle's lead B-25 flashed over the Japanese coastline, there were in the air exactly three obsolete Mitsubishi Type-96 fighters, with open cockpits and fixed landing

gear. Assigned to the Kasumigaura Air Corps, they circled ineffec-
tually over their home field at ten thousand feet, while two similar
vintage fighters waited on the runway.

Commander Masatake Okumiya (today a colonel, and chief of
intelligence for Japan Joint Chief of Staff) was an air staff officer
of the 11th Combined Air Flotilla, with headquarters at the
Kasumigaura Air Corps base, some twenty-five miles north of
Tokyo. Okumiya witnessed part of the raid, watching a B-25 skimming low over the ground near his headquarters.

Colonel Okumiya told me: "It was not until 1 p.m. that we
received official word at Kasumigaura that American planes were
over the mainland, flying very fast and low, and widely scattered.
The bomber tactics were superb. Their low-level approach caught
our air defense system completely unaware, and the three obsolete
fighters never even saw the B-25s.

Doolittle's bomber was the first to flash over Japan: people
along the coastline and in boats waved gaily to the planes as they
thundered in only twenty feet above the water. Each plane then followed an evasive course toward its target, flying down valleys and
buzzing the lowlands to elude any Japanese fighters which might be
waiting for them.

Doolittle reached Tokyo as the Japanese trooped into buildings
during an air raid drill, which through sheer coincidence was being
held at that moment.

Not until Doolittle's bomber released its 512 incendiary bombs
and was speeding away toward China did the Japanese sound the
alarm. But by now the other planes were hard after their targets,
skimming over the treetops until they climbed rapidly to escape the
blast of their own bombs.

Lieutenant Travis Hoover led his flight of three bombers over
Tokyo right on the heels of Doolittle's departing plane. From nine
hundred feet the three B-25s unloaded nine five-hundred-pound

high explosive bombs and three five-hundred-pound incendiary clusters, hitting targets in the northern area of Japan's largest city.

Captain David M. Jones took his element over the center part of Tokyo, while Captain Edward J. York bombed the southern part of the city after skimming over Tokyo Bay. A fourth flight commanded by Captain Greening struck at Kanagawa, Yokohama, and Yokosuka.

One after the other the bombers checked off their targets: a tank factory, a shipyard, docks, railroad yards, a steel plant, a gunpowder factory. At the Yokosuka naval base, a five-hundred-pounder from Lieutenant Edgar E. McElroy's bomber smashed into the carrier *Ryubo* as it lay in drydock.

The raid was coming off with spectacular success, but now the Japanese were trying hard to make up for their early blunders. More than thirty fighters ripped after the fast-flying Mitchells. The bomber gunners were ready and waiting, and their tracers sent several fighters to the ground.

Because of the heavy interception of the follow-up planes, Captain Greening kept his own bomber as low to the ground as possible. He hit his target, a gasoline refinery, right on the nose, but he was so low when the bombs exploded that the Mitchell was engulfed in a gigantic sheet of flame. The force of the explosion hurled the bomber almost out of control, and Greening and his co-pilot were slammed by the blast against the top of the cockpit.

Greening particularly had a hard time. Despite the fact that his gunners flamed two fighters, the Zeros hung tenaciously to his tail. In a desperate bid to elude his pursuers, Greening flew so low his propellers almost scraped the ground. During one high-speed run down a valley, fighters hard on his tail, he sent the bomber screaming beneath power lines in the hope that the fighters would smash into the cables.

South of Tokyo, the last flight of three B-25s scattered for individual attacks against Kobe, Osaka, and Nagoya. The sluggishness of the Japanese warning system paid extra dividends for these crews. Though Doolittle had hit Tokyo an hour before, not a fighter plane intercepted the three southernmost raiders. Each of the planes carried four five-hundred-pound incendiary clusters, with one hundred twenty-eight bombs to each cluster. The day was bright and clear, and the Mitchells hurled their bombs into their targets with high precision.

Not one plane was lost to enemy action, and only one ship sustained heavy damage. But from this point on, good fortune deserted the intrepid fliers. The attack against Japan proved to be the easiest part of the venture; the real hazards appeared during the escape flight to China.

The planes flew into increasingly severe storms of high winds and lashing rain. Fuel dwindled rapidly, and darkness made flying perilous. Fierce headwinds battered the Mitchells, cutting down their forward speed. Over China, facing saw-toothed mountain peaks, most of the planes were forced to climb to six and ten thousand feet, further draining their meager fuel.

There was only one break. On the last leg of the trip the wind reversed and each plane picked up speed. "Otherwise," Doolittle said later, "none of us would have reached China."

Finally the end came. One after the other the bombers crash-landed, or were abandoned by their crews. Fifty men leaped into pitch-black space over unknown territory, possibly enemy-held. Of these, only one man, Corporal L. D. Faktor, was killed. The others reached ground safely, a miraculous feat considering the circumstances. These forty-nine men, plus ten others who crash-landed along the coast, were saved by friendly Chinese.

Captain York landed his bomber twenty-five miles north of Vladivostok, where he and his four crewmen were interned by friendly Russians.

The two remaining bombers crashed in Japanese-held Chinese

territory, killing two of the ten men outright in the landing attempts. The eight who survived were to realize the worst fears they had held concerning the possibility of their capture.

For fifty-six days the Japanese continually beat and tortured the eight men. They spit questions at them without let-up. After nearly two months of intense physical and mental punishment, the eight fliers were returned to Shanghai's notorious Bridge House prison for "continued treatment."

On October 15, 1942, the Japanese marched three men—Farrow, Hallmark, and Spatz—to a Shanghai cemetery. Here the men were strapped to white crosses before shallow graves—and shot.

Four of the five surviving prisoners lived in hell for the long months until the war ended. The fifth, Lieutenant Robert J. Meder, died of starvation and beatings in late 1943 in a filthy cell in Nanking. The others spent all but seventy days of the next forty months in solitary confinement, and never did they communicate with the outside world during their inhuman treatment.

So ended the historic Doolittle raid against Japan.

There was never a second attempt at this type of raid. Sixteen bombers and two full crews were too high a price to pay for a slap against Japan. The enemy's cities were spared until the B-29s arrived to turn them into gigantic funeral pyres.

But in 1942 the price was well worth the results. The psychological effect upon Americans at home and overseas was tremendous. To some small degree, we had avenged Pearl Harbor. Most of all, we had shoved down the Japanese throat their proudest boast—that Tokyo could never be bombed.

★ ★ ★

Martin Caidin wrote during the second half of the twentieth century. He is renowned as a military historian.

★
★   IT IS FATAL TO ENTER ANY
★
      WAR WITHOUT THE WILL TO

      WIN IT.

                    —GEN. DOUGLAS MACARTHUR

VOYAGE TO FAITH

THOMAS FLEMING

They were stranded in the middle of the ocean, the nearest land perhaps a thousand miles away. In the terrible days that followed, their clothing disintegrated and the merciless sun and salt water combined to assault their bodies with ulcers.

Where was God?

Rickenbacker refused to give up on His protective care.

The miraculous story of how the Rickenbacker party survived at sea has proved to be perhaps the most enduring survival story ever written.

★ ★ ★

"Do you mind if I pray?" asked navigator Johnny DeAngelis as the plane began to fall into the ocean.

Copilot Jim Whittaker almost told him to shut up. Prayer was synonymous with weakness as far as he was concerned. Only brains and nerve were going to get them out of this mess.

"Five feet!" Eddie Rickenbacker barked in Whittaker's ear. "Three feet . . . One foot. Cut it!"

Whittaker pulled the mainline switch, knocking out all the electrical connections in the hurtling Army Air Corps B-17 Flying Fortress. Pilot Bill Cherry pancaked the big plane in the exact center of a trough between two huge Pacific swells.

The shock of the ninety-mile-an-hour impact was terrific. Whittaker thought his seat belt would slice him in two. But the five-man crew and their three passengers managed to scramble out of the sinking plane with only minor injuries. Inflating three yellow rafts, they tied them together with a long towline.

They had no idea where they were. The plane's navigational equipment had failed as they flew southwest from Hawaii, and they had tried to determine their location until they ran out of gas. The nearest land might be more than one thousand miles away. Their only hope was that a combined air-sea search by the U. S. Navy would respond to the SOS radioman Jimmy Reynolds had repeatedly flashed as they ditched.

The ditching had occurred at 4:30 p.m. on October 21, 1942, ten and a half months after the Japanese attack on Pearl Harbor. Two of the passengers were Eddie Rickenbacker and his friend Colonel Hans Adamson, who were on their way to the South Pacific to inspect American airfields. The third man, Sergeant Alex Kaczmarczyk, was returning to his regiment after a seven-week bout with jaundice.

They had no water; their only food was four oranges. Their only equipment was two sets of oars, some sheath knives, a few fishhooks and some line that one of them had snatched from a parachute kit before he quit the plane.

During the night the soaked men shivered in the tiny rafts,

which seemed to maintain five inches of water in their bottoms no matter how much they bailed. In the morning the tropic sun rose. All around them they saw the dorsal fins of circling sharks.

Their hopes plunged as the day passed with no sign of a search plane. By nightfall they were in agony from thirst. The second day was more of the same. Toward the end of that day, Whittaker noticed the plane's engineer, red-haired Johnny Bartek, was reading a khaki-covered New Testament he had taken from his pocket.

On the fourth day they were down to their last orange. Their hunger was agonizing. They began talking about cutting off fingers or toes to use as bait on their fishhooks. Suddenly a sea swallow, a bird about half the size of a seagull, landed on Eddie Rickenbacker's head. Within seconds it was seized and its raw flesh distributed among the rafts. They used the bird's intestines as bait and quickly caught several small fish, which they sliced up and shared the same way.

This did not solve their water problem. If anything, the raw fish intensified their thirst. Johnny Bartek wondered if they ought to have a prayer meeting. Whittaker had no enthusiasm for the idea. But Rickenbacker, a man who had survived countless aerial combats and a harrowing commercial-plane crash, agreed. They pulled the rafts together and Colonel Adamson, as the senior officer, was asked to read from Bartek's New Testament.

He read from Matthew, the sixth chapter, the thirty-first to the thirty-fourth verses: "Therefore take no thought, saying, "What shall we eat? or, What shall we drink? or, Wherewithal shall we be clothed? . . . For your heavenly Father knoweth that ye have need of all these things. . . . Take therefore no thought for the morrow. . . . Sufficient unto the day is the evil thereof."

Jim Whittaker remarked wryly that the evil had certainly been sufficient for the last three days. He had been exposed to Bible teaching as a boy in Missouri, but for most of his life he had been disdainful of religion. He felt God had never done much for him.

So why should he worship? After another miserable night in the rafts, Whittaker dismissed the verses from Matthew with the bitter thought that he would believe them when he saw some food and drink.

They began and ended the sixth day with prayer services and more readings from Bartek's New Testament. Whittaker, now almost mad from hunger and thirst, could barely restrain his contempt. Suddenly he heard Pilot Bill Cherry praying directly to God.

"Old Master," he said, "we know there isn't a guarantee we'll eat in the morning. But we're in an awful fix. We sure are counting on a little something by the day after tomorrow, at least. See what you can do, Old Master."

After the prayer, Cherry performed another evening ritual. He fired a flare from a Very pistol into the darkening sky, hoping it would attract a search plane. Several of the flares had been duds. This one malfunctioned and fell back, into the sea, where it zigzagged around them, burning brightly. A school of good-sized fish were attracted by the light and attacked by barracuda. Two of the hunted fish leaped out of the water and landed in Whittaker's raft. They were quickly killed and sliced up for distribution.

All right, Whittaker told himself. God—or luck—had sent them food. But it was lack of water that was going to kill them long before they starved to death.

The eighth evening, at their prayer service, Billy Cherry asked the "Old Master" specifically for water. The men could not survive another day without it.

As they wallowed into another choppy, chilling twilight, Whittaker noticed a cloud on their left beginning to change from fleecy white to darkish blue. A curtain of rain descended on the sea and began moving toward them.

"Thanks, Old Master!" Bill Cherry cried as the squall deluged them with sheets of cold, drinkable water. They caught the rain in their hands and poured it down their parched throats. They held up their shirts and rung water from them into their Mae West life jackets, to build up a reserve.

Whittaker worked at saving the water as frantically as the rest of them, while within his soul a spiritual earthquake took place. God had answered Cherry's prayers. Was it time for Whittaker to start praying too?

The next morning the sun scorched them again. As the ninth and tenth days passed with no rescuers, one man begged God to kill him. Rickenbacker took charge. "Cut that out!" he roared. "Don't bother him with that whining! He answers *men's* prayers."

When Rickenbacker prayed, he asked God to do specific things: Guide the rescuers to them, help them reach land. Once he added: "You, our Father, know we are not asking you to do it all. We will help ourselves, if you will give us a chance."

On the eleventh day another cloud darkened and spilled rain on them. Again they gulped the water as it came down, and frantically tried to save some of it. As the squall intensified, it tipped over the smallest raft, in which Sergeant Kaczmarczyk was riding. When the men got him into one of the bigger rafts, they realized he was dying. He had never uttered a word of complaint throughout the ordeal. He died the next night and they recited prayers for his soul and released his body to the depths.

On the thirteenth day the sun still scorched them. Rain began falling about a mile away, but the wind veered and it moved away from them. "God," Jim Whittaker prayed aloud, "you know what that water means to us. It is in your power to send back that rain." Some men scoffed at this plea. Whittaker himself was amazed by the words that had leaped from his lips. But he accepted them, confessing the birth of faith in his proud, lonely soul.

The bluish-black curtain of water began moving toward them —*against the wind!* Within minutes, it was drenching the rafts.

On the morning of the fourteenth day the wind died completely.

They were in the doldrums. By this time, everyone's lower body was a mass of saltwater ulcers. Their clothing had disintegrated and the sun began to inflict serious burns. The water had also rotted the fishing lines and the sharks had snapped them off. The men were living on a few sips of water a day.

Only Rickenbacker refused to give up. He berated anyone who said a discouraging word. At the prayer service that ended the four-teenth day, he led them in asking God for wind to blow them out of the doldrums.

No wind appeared. Instead, on the eighteenth and nineteenth days came blows that would have destroyed them, if they had not built up their courage with those hours of daily prayer.

At twilight on the eighteenth day, a search plane passed within three miles without sighting them. Rickenbacker insisted that if the plane came once, it could come again. It returned twice—and missed them both times.

Some of the men groaned and almost despaired, but Jim Whittaker did not join them. As he thought of the amazing answers to so many of their prayers, he became convinced that God was not going to abandon them.

On the twentieth day they decided to separate to give the search planes a better chance of spotting them. Although another plane flew close and failed to see them, Whittaker still felt strangely hope-ful. The next morning Johnny DeAngelis shook Whittaker awake and pointed toward the horizon. "It may be a mirage, but I think I see something."

It was a line of palm trees. Whittaker began rowing toward them. Neither DeAngelis nor Jimmy Reynolds was strong enough to sit up, much less row. Whittaker himself, before he saw those trees, had been so weak he could not have bent a pin. Yet he some-how found the strength to row for seven and a half hours.

Finally the island was only two hundred fifty yards away. The palm trees swayed invitingly. With no warning a current seized the raft and swept them a mile offshore.

"God," Whittaker prayed, "give me a little more strength."

He went back to rowing. Rain descended, soaking and invigorating him, but making it hard to find the island. Then a 12-foot-long gray form slid under the raft and slashed at an oar. Another shark bumped the raft, trying to upset it.

"God!" cried Whittaker. "Don't quit me now."

Almost instantly he felt strength surge in his arms and shoulders. The rain continued to sluice down in torrents. The sharks continued to attack. But Whittaker rowed past them, oblivious. Ahead lay one more danger: a reef. But swells lifted them over the jagged stone teeth and minutes later, the raft touched land.

Soon friendly natives helped them to their huts and notified the U.S. Navy. They learned search planes had rescued Bill Cherry, Rickenbacker and the others. When Jim Whittaker recovered from his ordeal, he went home to tell his story to defense workers across America.

"I told them how during those blazing days I found my God." He vowed to tell it again and again as long as he lived, because it was "the greatest story a man can tell."

★ ★ ★

Thomas Fleming wrote during the second half of the twentieth century.

★ IT IS NOT ENOUGH TO FIGHT.
★ IT IS THE SPIRIT WHICH WE
★ BRING TO THE FIGHT THAT
DECIDES THE ISSUE. IT IS
MORALE THAT WINS THE
VICTORY.

—GEORGE CATLETT MARSHALL

THE LOST FORTRESS

ERNIE PYLE

No American war correspondent has ever been more loved and mourned than Ernie Pyle, author of *Here Is Your War, Brave Men* and *Last Chapter*. Pyle was famous for his columns extolling the common soldier and sharing his lot, whatever the conditions. He paid the supreme price himself in the battle for Okinawa during World War II.

Typical of his empathizing heart poured onto paper is this story. The setting: an airfield at sunset in North Africa.

★ ★ ★

George Mehko, who miraculously survived twenty-five B-17 bombing missions, had this to say about what it was like to be on such a flight. "Only two to three of every ten survived the war. We tended not to make strong friendships because so few returned alive from these bombing missions. Knowing the odds, we'd look around the breakfast table and think, *Out of the ten of us, only two will remain alive. I wonder which of us will be those two?* Inside the plane, being it was only nine feet across, quarters were cramped. Most cramped of all were the ball-turret gunners. They were also the coldest. At our top cruising elevation of twenty-six to twenty-eight thousand feet it was 45 degrees below zero in the plane, so we had to wear heavily padded suits wired to extension cords to avoid freezing to death. Most of us got frostbite on the exposed parts of our faces. The flights usually lasted nine hours, but we only had oxygen for six—and no sanitary facilities at all! Because the noise of the engines was so deafening, communication between crew members was extremely difficult. It was anything but romantic!" (Address to Conifer, CO Kiwanis, May 31, 2006).

★ ★ ★

It was late afternoon at our desert airdrome. The sun was lazy, the air was warm, and a faint haze of propeller dust hung over the field, giving it softness. It was time for the planes to start coming back from their mission, and one by one they did come—high-flying Fortresses and fiery little Lightnings. Nobody paid a great deal of attention, for this returning was a daily, routine thing.

Finally they were all in—all, that is, except one. Operations reported a Fortress missing. Returning pilots said it had lagged behind and lost altitude just after leaving the target. The last report said the Fortress couldn't stay in the air more than five minutes. Hours had passed since then. So it was gone.

Ten men were in that plane. The day's accomplishments had been great, but the thought of ten lost friends cast a pall over us. We had already seen death that afternoon. One of the returning Fortresses had released a red flare over the field, and I had stood with others beneath the great plane as they handed its dead pilot, head downward, through the escape hatch onto a stretcher.

The faces of his crew were grave, and nobody talked very loud. One man clutched a leather cap with blood on it. The pilot's hands were very white. Everybody knew the pilot. He was so young, a couple of hours before. The war came inside us then, and we felt it deeply.

After the last report, half a dozen of us went to the high control tower. We went there every evening, for two things—to watch the sunset, and to get word on the progress of the German bombers that frequently came just after dusk to blast our airdrome.

The sunsets in the desert are truly things with souls. The violence of their color is incredible. They splatter the sky and the clouds with a surging beauty. The mountains stand dark against the horizon, and palm trees silhouette themselves dramatically against the fiery west.

As we stood on the tower looking down over this scene, the day began folding itself up. Fighter planes, which had patrolled the field all day, were coming in. All the soldiers in the tent camps had finished supper. That noiseless peace that sometimes comes just before dusk hung over the airdrome. Men talked in low tones about the dead pilot and the lost Fortress. We thought we would wait a few minutes more to see if the Germans were coming over.

And then an electric thing happened. Far off in the dusk a red flare shot into the sky. It made an arc against the dark background of the mountains and fell to the earth. It couldn't be anything else. It had to be. The ten dead men were coming home!

"Where's the flare gun? Gimme a green flare!" yelled an officer.

He ran to the edge of the tower, shouted, "Look out below!" and fired a green rocket into the air. Then we saw the plane—just a tiny black speck. It seemed almost on the ground, it was so low, and in the first glance we could sense that it was barely moving, barely staying in the air. Crippled and alone, two hours behind all the rest, it was dragging itself home.

I was a layman, and no longer of the fraternity that flies, but I could feel. And at that moment I felt something close to human love for that faithful, battered machine, that far, dark speck struggling toward us with such pathetic slowness.

All of us stood tense, hardly remembering anyone else was there. With all our nerves we seemed to pull the plane toward us. I suspect a photograph would have shown us all leaning slightly to the left. Not one of us thought the plane would ever make the field, but on it came—so slowly that it was cruel to watch.

It reached the far end of the airdrome, still holding its pathetic little altitude. It skimmed over the tops of parked planes, and kept on, actually reaching out—it seemed to us—for the runway. A few hundred yards more now. Could it? Would it? Was it truly possible?

They cleared the last plane, they were over the runway. They settled slowly. The wheels touched softly. And as the plane rolled on down the runway the thousands of men around that vast field suddenly realized that they were weak and that they could hear their hearts pounding.

The last of the sunset died, and the sky turned into blackness, which would help the Germans if they came on schedule with their bombs. But nobody cared. Our ten dead men were miraculously back from the grave.

And what a story they had to tell! Nothing quite like it had happened before in this war.

The Tripoli airdrome, which was their target, was heavily defended, by both fighter planes and antiaircraft guns. Flying into that hailstorm, as one pilot said, was like a mouse attacking a dozen cats.

The *Thunderbird*—for that was the name of their Fortress—was first hit just as it dropped its bomb load. One engine went out. Then a few moments later the other engine on the same side went. When both engines went out on the same side it was usually fatal. And therein lay the difference of that feat from other instances of bringing damaged bombers home.

The *Thunderbird* was forced to drop below the other Fortresses. And the moment a Fortress dropped down or lagged behind, German fighters were on it like vultures. The boys didn't know how many Germans were in the air, but they thought there must have been thirty.

Our Lightning fighters, escorting the Fortress, stuck by the *Thunderbird* and fought as long as they could, but finally they had to leave or they wouldn't have had enough fuel to make it home; the last fighter left the crippled Fortress about forty miles from Tripoli. Fortunately, the swarm of German fighters started home at the same time, for their gas was low too.

The *Thunderbird* flew on another twenty miles. Then a single German fighter appeared, and dived at them. Its guns did great damage to the already crippled plane, but simply couldn't knock it out of the air.

Finally the fighter ran out of ammunition, and left. Our boys were alone with their grave troubles. Two engines were gone, most of the guns were out of commission, and they were still more than four hundred miles from home. The radio was out. They were losing altitude, five hundred feet a minute—and then they were down to two thousand.

The pilot called up his crew and held a consultation. Did they want to jump? They all said they would ride the plane as long as it was in the air. He decided to keep going. The ship was completely out of trim, cocked over at a terrible angle. But they gradually got it trimmed so that it stopped losing altitude.

By then they were down to nine hundred feet, and a solid wall of mountains ahead barred the way homeward. They flew along parallel to those mountains for a long time, but they were then miraculously gaining some altitude. Finally they got the thing to fifteen hundred feet.

The lowest pass was sixteen hundred feet, but they came across at fifteen hundred. Explain that if you can! Maybe it was as the pilot said: "We didn't come over the mountains, we came through them."

The copilot said, "I was blowing on the windshield trying to push her along. Once I almost wanted to reach a foot down and sort of walk us along over the pass."

And the navigator said, "If I had been on the wingtip, I could have touched the ground with my hand when we went through the pass."

The air currents were bad. One wing was cocked away down. It was hard to hold. The pilots had a horrible fear that the low wing would drop clear down and they'd roll over and go into a spin. But they didn't. The navigator came into the cockpit, and he and the pilots navigated the plane home. Never for a second could they feel any real assurance of making it. They were practically rigid, but they talked a blue streak all the time—and cussed, as airmen do.

Everything seemed against them. The gas consumption doubled, squandering their precious supply. To top off their misery, they had a bad headwind. The gas gauge went down and down.

At last the navigator said they were only forty miles from home, but those forty miles passed as though they were driving a horse and buggy. Dusk, coming down on the sandy haze, made the vast flat desert an indefinite thing. One oasis looked exactly like another. But they knew when they were near home. Then they shot their red flare and waited for the green flare from our control tower. A minute later it came—the most beautiful sight that crew had ever seen.

When the plane touched the ground they cut the switches and let it roll. For it had no brakes. At the end of the roll the big Fortress veered off the side of the runway. It climaxed its historic homecoming by spinning madly around five times and then running backwards for fifty yards before it stopped. When they checked the gas gauges, they found one tank dry and the other down to twenty gallons.

Deep dusk enveloped the field. Five more minutes and they never would have found it. The weary, crippled Fortress had flown for the incredible time of four and one-half hours on one pair of motors. Any pilot will tell you it's impossible.

That night, with the pilot and some of the crew, we drank a toast. One visitor raised his glass, "Here's to your safe return." But the pilot raised his own glass and said instead, "Here's to a *#&* good airplane!" And the others of the crew raised their glasses and repeated, "Here's to a *#&* good airplane!"

Perhaps the real climax was that during the agonizing homeward crawl, that one crippled plane shot down the fantastic total of six German fighters. The score was officially confirmed.

★ ★ ★

Ernie Pyle (1900–1945) was America's most-beloved World War II war correspondent, author of Ernie Pyle in England *(1941),* Here Is Your War *(1943),* Brave Men *(1944), and* Last Chapter *(1946). He was killed in the South Pacific. For his war reporting he was awarded the* Pulitzer Prize *(1942).*

★
★
★

A SHIP IS ALWAYS REFERRED
TO AS A 'SHE' BECAUSE IT
COSTS SO MUCH TO KEEP ONE
IN PAINT AND POWDER.

—GEN. CHESTER WILLIAM NIMITZ

THE DRESDEN
INFERNO

ANNE WAHLE
(WITH ROUL TUNLEY)

D resden was called "Florence on the Elbe" and was one of
the world's most beautiful cities, an art center considered
off-limits to Allied bombing during World War II. By
early 1945 it housed more than six hundred thousand people,
including scores of Allied prisoners-of-war and refugees from all
over Europe. So safe did its residents feel, in fact, that its antiaircraft
guns had been removed.

But in the waning months of the war, the Allied high command
decided to use mass terror on cities to help bring an end to the war.
So it was on the night of February 13, 1945, that nearly eight hundred British Lancasters bombed unsuspecting Dresden, mostly with
incendiaries. The next day, three hundred U.S. Flying Fortresses finished the job. This attack turned out to be one of the greatest disas-
ters of all time. In minutes, that new and deadly invention of World
War II—a firestorm—was under way. It was the biggest ever dealt.

It sucked oxygen from the air-raid shelters; it fanned a tornado, which ripped off clothes and blew people into treetops; and it generated heat so intense that it shrank bodies to half their size without touching them with flame. No one can ever know for sure, but it is estimated that one hundred thirty-five thousand people perished—more than in Hiroshima.

No other World War II bombing incident caused more public outrage than this one. It was as though the Allies had deliberately bombed St. Peter's Cathedral, the Parthenon, or the Taj Mahal. The American novelist and essayist Kurt Vonnegut was also in Dresden on that date. From this horrific experience he created his literary masterpiece, *Slaughterhouse Five*.

It so happened that Anne Wahle, the American wife of an Austrian diplomat who had recently been poisoned by the Nazis, was there in the city with her children (Dick, 14; Noonie, 11; and Elizabeth, 1), Hilda (a maid), and a German captain (a boarder), when the planes flew over. Following is her description of the experience.

★ ★ ★

I was suddenly yanked back to the present by the sound of an air-raid alarm. I looked at my watch. It was 9:35 p.m. The siren made us more tense than frightened, since we'd had a number of alarms during the last few months but no serious raids.

We generally had about ten minutes before the planes reached the area—enough time to get the children and the tenants from the upper floors into the shelter, but no time to waste. First I woke Noonie and told her to hurry. Then I went to my room and hastily dressed for the shelter in an old brown wool dress and tweed coat. Because I didn't want to wear my pumps in the cellar, I slipped stockingless into a pair of Dick's old shoes that were standing in the hallway. They were full of holes and too big for me, but I thought they'd be good enough. The alerts were usually short.

In the nursery, Elizabeth was sleeping peacefully in her crib. While I woke and dressed her, I kept thinking about Dick. I felt panicky that he was not home at such a time. One never knew when an alert might turn into the real thing. Well, there was nothing I could do about it.

Finally Elizabeth was ready. I put her in the baby carriage, and stuffed clean diapers in, as well as several bottles of Nestlé's milk, a loaf of bread, and all the cigarettes (almost as valuable as gold during those war years) we possessed. I also gathered up three suitcases bulging with all sorts of necessities—clothing, needles and thread, first-aid kit, toilet paper, a precious bar of soap. They were always packed for just such an emergency.

By this time, Hilda and the captain were dressed and ready. The other tenants were already in the shelter. The captain and I carried the carriage down the short flight of steps and closed the heavy door. We all took our seats on the benches in the small room.

In all, there were twelve of us in the cellar that night: Elizabeth, Hilda, the captain, and myself from the first floor; the elderly Jewish widow and a middle-aged housewife, Frau Bostel, who had apartments on the second floor; and two spinsters and the concierge's wife with two small children who lived on the third floor. As we sat waiting, all I could think of was Dick. I hoped he was safe in the school shelter.

We didn't have long to wait. First we heard the distant thunder of planes and the subsequent whine of bombs, followed by explosions as they hit. We all huddled together instinctively at each crash even though we'd heard this sound before.

Then suddenly something new happened. The roar grew much louder, more insistent. Instantly we found ourselves on a new level of fear. As the terror mounted, we looked at each other in the flickering light of the candle. It had never been like this before. Soon the noise grew deafening. We knew we were in the center of an attack.

This was it! Hundreds of bombs were falling around us like a thousand hells. This was no raid on peripheral targets like the others. This was an all-out attempt to destroy the city itself—the front-line attack I had so long feared.

I glanced up at the ceiling, which vibrated with every crash. I wondered if it would hold. Only *I* knew it could not withstand an explosive bomb. I was glad the others didn't know. All of us sat, rigid as statues, not daring to move except to draw imperceptibly closer from time to time. Noonie crouched at my knees, sobbing and burying her head in my lap. Some prayed. All of us except Elizabeth expected death at any moment. She slept soundly in my arms, oblivious to everything.

The pounding lasted twenty-four minutes. It seemed like twenty-four years. But finally the roaring and the screeching subsided as the planes turned back. Shortly afterward, we heard a distant all-clear. It was very faint. Apparently most of the sirens had been knocked out.

After a few minutes, the captain and I decided to investigate. Moving up the steps, we cautiously opened the heavy door and stepped into the vestibule. Through the front door, the whole city shone a brilliant orange. Everything was aflame, with a hurricane wind swirling sparks around like fiery snowflakes. The trees, the wall, the asphalt in the road, the houses around us—all were burning.

Miraculously, our house seemed spared, at least on the inside. The captain and I ran upstairs to check the most important part— the roof. We found it full of holes where the tiles had been broken, and here and there the attic floor had been charred by flying sparks, but nothing had actually caught fire. With luck we might save it. We ran down to the basement to tell the others the good news and to organize a water brigade to keep the top floor from igniting. The elderly widow looked after the children while the rest of us grabbed pails and pots to carry water.

For an hour we feverishly poured water on the spots that were catching fire from the sparks that came through the roof holes. Up and down we ran until the roof seemed out of danger. The exertion was exhausting because the air seemed to hold so little oxygen. We panted like race horses.

Finally the frenzy of the fires slackened somewhat. The winds also died down and there seemed less danger of suffocation. I took the opportunity to return to the cellar and check the children. To my surprise and joy, I found Dick there. He was sprawled on the floor in the corner, his eyes closed. I ran over and kneeled down beside him. His breathing was regular, and he didn't have any wounds or cuts that I could see. Even his glasses were unbroken.

I took his hand in mine, and he opened his eyes. "Are you all right?" I asked. He nodded without saying anything. "Thank God you're safe!" I breathed. He stared at me without smiling, and his eyes looked hollow and far away. I stayed there, watching him for a while. He didn't seem to have any injuries, at least physical, and I could only guess at what had happened. Dick was an unusually sensitive boy, and the ordeal of reaching home through the holocaust had probably rendered him speechless. Satisfied that he was all right physically, I didn't press him further. He would speak when he could. I turned my attention to the other children. Elizabeth, bless her, was still fast asleep in her carriage, and Noonie, too, was now slumbering on a pile of blankets.

I returned to the attic. The captain and Hilda were watching for sparks and burning twigs that still fell through the roof occasionally, and Frau Bostel and the two spinsters were supplying them with water. Things seemed so well under control, I asked Hilda to help me check our apartment.

Although all the electricity was off, we had no trouble making our way from room to room. Everything was brightly lit by the flames from the still-burning city. All windows, of course, were out. The glass had been shattered by the explosions and by the hurricane winds generated by the firestorm. Draperies and curtains were in shreds. But the rooms and the furniture were still there, and we felt lucky.

"Shall we bring up the children and put them to bed?" asked Hilda.

"No, leave them there a little longer,"I said. "The fire might frighten them."

This was not my real reason for leaving them in the shelter. I knew the bombers would return, but I didn't want to alarm Hilda by saying so. She had already had several hysterical fits of crying.

Having been in the Hamburg raid [fifty thousand had died in that one] and having read everything I could about bombings, I had learned the routine. After the first strike there was always too much smoke, fire, and debris for the attackers to see clearly what had been done. After a while, when things had settled somewhat, the bombers would return to finish the job.

As Hilda and I walked through the rooms, the clutter was overwhelming. High winds had overturned tables and chairs, knocked down pictures, scattered twigs and branches from the tree in the garden, and left bits of silk and damask from the curtains on the floor. Hilda began straightening things, picking up pieces of material she wanted to salvage. It seemed so useless I couldn't watch her do it. Finally I said, "Don't bother, Hilda. The bombers will return any minute." She looked at me as though I'd gone out of my mind, but she didn't say anything.

The captain finally joined us in the living room. He looked exhausted, as much from the terrifying raid as from the breath-consuming exertion of carrying buckets up and down stairs. We all dropped into chairs and couches. No one spoke. The scene was an eerie one, with the three of us—our faces lit up by the flames outside—sitting around waiting for what appeared to be certain death. I had no illusions about the sanctuary of our little, fire-ringed island. As the minutes ticked away, I was sure the bombers would return. And this time might well be the end.

Some time after one o'clock, the second attack began. We had almost no warning. Although the first raid had been trumpeted by a loud blare of sirens, now the signal was barely audible. The sirens were still out.

We hurried down to the shelter, wondering if this was the coup de grâce. Even before we'd had time to shut the door properly, the planes were upon us. With an unearthly roar, hundreds of bombs shrieked down. The explosions were on all sides of us now, louder, heavier, more concentrated than the first attack.

As bomb after bomb crashed around us, we sat congealed in terror, clinging to life as long as we could. Finally, there was an ear-splitting sound, and the shelter moved. The candle fell off the box it was on, and we were plunged into total darkness. I knew a bomb had hit the house.

It was the first time I'd felt anything like it. But when I recovered from the initial shock, I realized it sounded more like an incendiary than an explosive bomb. My suspicion was confirmed when I saw a red glow beneath the cellar door. Seeing that the bomb had hit so close to the entrance made my heart skip a beat. Were we trapped? But before I could even think about it, another bomb hit the house . . . and another . . . and another. Each time the shelter moved, I knew we had been hit, but I didn't know if the others understood. It seemed twice as bad to die in the darkness, and so I groped on the floor, found the candle and lit it again. The first face my eyes fell on was the captain's. From his expression I could tell he knew what had happened, but he looked remarkably calm all the same. I decided to try to be like him. If I panicked, I knew we'd have no chance.

The bombs that hit the house seemed to mark the raid's climax. Shortly after, the roar began to die down. But this time, as the planes turned back, there was no all-clear. Not even a faint one. All sirens had obviously been knocked out.

I looked around at the occupants in the cellar. Everybody *looked* all right—at least within the confines of our tiny room. We waited a few more minutes until the attack seemed definitely over, and then the captain and I cautiously approached the shelter door. The red glow at the doorsill had grown dimmer and we decided to open the door. Very slowly we pushed it back a little. As we did so, a hot, suffocating, phosphorous smoke rushed in, almost choking us to death. We slammed the door shut fast.

It was too soon to venture out, but how long dared we wait? The house was undoubtedly burning after those incendiaries, and we couldn't wait too long. There was a good chance of its collapsing on top of us and burying us all alive. We had no idea how much time we had before this would happen.

As we waited, my heart pounded and I could feel my pulse hammering at my eardrums. It was an agonizing few minutes. Every moment I expected the house to fall in on us. Finally, when I could stand it no longer, we opened the door again—very slowly. This time we'd protected ourselves with helmets and gas masks, and the smoke didn't bother us. We closed the door quickly behind us to protect the cellar.

Standing in the vestibule, the captain and I looked through the front door directly into an inferno. I had never seen anything like it. Howling gusts of hurricane force whipped flames in all directions. Nothing seemed to be spared. I watched little trains of flame race along garden paths and suddenly ignite a tree or even a stone ornament. A neighbor's house that had survived the first attack now crumbled to the ground with a roar, sending up huge clouds of thick red dust into the orange flames.

Terrified that our house would collapse too, I took a deep breath behind my mask, braced myself, and stepped out into the gale just far enough to see what was happening to the upper stories. I saw that the house was completely aflame at the top and was rapidly burning down to the second floor. I tried to estimate the time it would take it to collapse, and figured we might have at least ten minutes to reach safety. *Safety!* The word had a mocking ring. Where could anyone find safety in this crumbling, dying city? I had no idea, but I knew anywhere was better than certain death in a cellar where we'd soon be buried alive under crashing bricks and burning beams. We had no chance at all there.

I went back into the cellar, followed by the captain. All eyes were upon us, awaiting the word. I knew I had to hide my panic, and as calmly as I could, said, "Don't be alarmed, but the house has been hit and can't be saved. It's burning, but we have a few minutes before it collapses. Just take your blankets, dip them in the tub of water, and wrap them around you. Put on your helmets, your gas masks. Pick up your suitcases and get out of here as fast as you can."

I was amazed that I sounded as calm as I did, and the fact that I could say *anything* helped lessen my panic. But my words didn't have the effect I'd hoped for at all . . .

At first there was death-like silence as everybody stared at me, stunned. Then suddenly bedlam took over as everybody bolted. Completely out of control, they raced back and forth like crazed animals. Finally in terror they stampeded the door and raced out into the burning city. All of them disappeared, even the elderly widow who was the last up the stairs. They took neither helmets, gas masks, nor wet blankets. They even left their suitcases behind.

Now it was my turn to be stunned. I watched with my mouth open. No one could possibly survive in that heat and fire without wet blankets and the other equipment, and the spectacle of these insane people rushing headlong to certain death froze me in my tracks. When I could recover from my horror long enough to shout at them, they had already gone. There was nothing I could do.

The only ones who remained behind were the captain, Hilda, the children, and myself. Frau Bostel had rushed out with the rest, but as I busied myself getting the children ready, she returned. She screamed that her eyes had been burned. At this point, I was in no mood to delay and sacrifice our lives for Frau Bostel's stupidity, but I was so struck by her obvious pain that I took the time to administer a boric acid solution I had in my medicine kit. She had probably been hit by the fumes from the phosphorous bombs. Then I quickly turned to the job of getting my family out. I had no idea where we were going, but I knew we had no time to lose getting there.

First, I lined up the children at the entrance, along with Hilda, while the captain stood outside and yelled back reports about the progress of the crumbling house. I made each one put on a helmet and gas mask, except Elizabeth. Then I dunked our blankets in the tub of water until they were well soaked, and wrapped one around each person. I closed the top of the carriage containing Elizabeth and threw a blanket over it. Finally, I threw a wet blanket around myself, almost collapsing under the weight. I was adjusting my gas mask just before leaving when Frau Bostel crawled up to me on her knees.

"Please, please!" she begged. "Take me along."

I had little sympathy for Frau Bostel. A buxom blonde, addicted to flashy clothes, dyed hair, and schnapps, I had once caught her stealing the only bottle of liquor we possessed. Worse, I had strong reason to suspect that she was the one who had tipped off the Gestapo about my feeding the elderly Jewish lady. But in spite of all this, I found it impossible to leave this human being alone—helpless, blinded, and in pain—to die in the cellar.

"Quick!" I said. "We have no time to lose."

With frantic speed, I got her ready as best I could while the captain in the vestibule yelled at us not to delay. Just before I adjusted her gas mask, I placed another well-soaked wad of gauze in front of her eyes. Because she had no vision at all, she had to be led.

Then, as I turned to go, there was another maddening hold-up. For some incredible reason, Hilda had taken off her gas mask and sneaked upstairs while I was busy with Frau Bostel. Now she came running back, screaming that her eyes had been injured. I was ready to explode.

"You'd better hurry!" shouted the captain from upstairs. "This house isn't going to stay together forever!"

Sharply, I told Hilda there was just no time to tend to her. She was to follow as best as she could. I'd help her as soon as possible.

The captain and I carried the carriage up the steps. When we reached the vestibule and were all together—each one holding his suitcase—we opened the front door and stepped out into the inferno. There was no sign of any of the others. They'd been swallowed by the burning city.

We made our way through the garden along the brick path that led to the street beyond—a distance of about one hundred fifty feet. But progress was painfully slow because of the raging winds, the flames, and the enormous weight of the wet blankets over our heads. We had gone about half way when a terrible thing happened. The wife of the concierge suddenly appeared before us, coming from the opposite direction. She was pushing an open baby carriage in which her two youngsters were sitting bolt upright like dolls. They were bareheaded with no protection whatsoever—no coats, no blankets, no helmets, no gas masks. She was wearing nothing but an old blue house dress. Wildly she raced past us, straight into the fire. Like something out of *die Götterdämmerung*, she and the children instantly disappeared in the flames. Although it was a scene I knew I'd never forget, such was the urgency of the moment that we never even stopped moving.

We made our way as fast as we could toward the street, but at each step the blankets seemed to grow heavier. The flames licked at our legs, and the flying sparks burned our exposed flesh. Any clothing not covered by the blankets was also burned. Frau Bostel, clinging to me, and Hilda, hanging on to her, made the going even slower. Both complained about their eyes, but there was nothing we could do at the moment. Since I was also wheeling the baby carriage, the captain was leading the children.

We reached the gate and turned into the street. Just as we did, two houses on the other side came crashing down with a gigantic roar, scattering dust and bricks. Fortunately the street was wide enough so that none of the debris hit us.

At this point, Dick remembered he'd left his suitcase standing in front of the house. He had put it there when helping Frau Bostel down the steps. For a moment, we thought of leaving it, but then we decided that if everybody waited in the street, Dick and I could go back for it. Besides, we'd forgotten our three bicycles in the garage. I felt we needed them.

Dick and I made our way back as quickly as we could, considering the heavy blankets and the swirling of the wind and flame. The suitcase was just where Dick had left it, still untouched by fire. He snatched it up and we moved toward the garage. The house was still standing, but it looked as though it would collapse any minute.

As we neared the garage, which was on the street, we saw a stranger dart in, grab a bicycle and ride away on it. It all happened in a matter of seconds. It was useless to shout at the thief (no voice would carry in that howling wind), much less try to catch him. Anyway, two bikes were still left, and these we wheeled along until we'd rejoined our group.

All of us pushed down the street again. The asphalt was sticky, and bits of burning twigs blown along gave it the look of a sea of flame. The heat was almost unbearable, and sudden gusts of wind made us grab at each other for fear of being blown away. It was almost impossible to see through the sparks that kept whirling around us like a red blizzard, but we kept peering through them for a sign of some kind of shelter.

Finally, through the storm, I saw a house that had not been hit. The windows were shattered of course, but otherwise it looked all right. It was not burning, and it appeared solid on its foundation. I steered our group toward it. When we reached the gate, I sent the women on ahead with the captain and the children so that I could better manipulate the bulky carriage down the narrow path. They went into the entrance hall and had no trouble finding the door to the cellar. We pushed it open without difficulty and walked part way down the steps. It was in total darkness, but when I used the flashlight we had with us, we saw the room was full of people. We asked if we could take shelter, and were invited to come in, baby carriage and all.

After the blazing hell of the streets with its raging winds, the cellar was like heaven—cool, quiet, and apparently safe from immediate danger. Gratefully, we groped our way down the rest of the steps and along a stone wall. We kept tripping over outstretched bodies. Finally we found a vacant place, and huddled there, glad to be alive.

The whimpering of Hilda and Frau Bostel was muted but constant. Both seemed to be suffering, but there was little I could do. I tried to ease their pain by changing their gauze pads frequently, working by the light of a candle. After about an hour, Hilda told me that her pain had subsided a bit, but Frau Bostel continued to cry softly into her woolen scarf.

By this time, I decided I wanted to take a look outside to see if things were any better. As I got up, the captain followed me. We both went up the steps into the street. There was a tremendous amount of heavy black smoke, but the flames and high winds of the firestorm had died down. There were only a few errant sparks in the air. Since I knew the children and Hilda were safe for the moment, I decided to go back to the house and see if there was anything I could salvage, especially a pair of my own shoes. Dick's were not very comfortable.

The captain went with me. It didn't take us as long to get back as it had taken to get away. As we approached the house, we saw that it had not yet collapsed. It had burned down to the first floor and our apartment was now ablaze. It seemed impossible to salvage anything, and so we just stood there. I watched the hissing flames devour everything we owned—the beautiful Biedermeyer furniture from my mother's family that I'd brought over from America, the family portraits, the books, the rugs—all going up in flames. But curiously, I watched them go without regret. My only emotion at that moment was one of relief. The family was safe—at least for the time being—and that was all that mattered.

While we stood there, the captain pointed to the far side of the apartment. The flames apparently had not yet reached this part, and it looked as though one or two rooms might be untouched. He told me he was going to see if he could save anything for us. "Please, don't," I begged. "The beams will fall on you!" But he was off before I could stop him. He disappeared inside the house.

As I waited, walls continued to tumble, beams fell, and spurts of flame shot out of the windows. What a mad gesture the captain had made! The firestorm had made everyone crazy. As the moments wore on, my anxiety increased, for the building had certainly swallowed him up.

At this point, I didn't know what to do. I rushed around all sides of the house, trying to get a glimpse of him. I blamed myself, feeling that somehow I should have stopped him. Minutes passed. I felt completely helpless. I couldn't go after him, but neither could I wait for him indefinitely, leaving my children in the shelter.

Then, just as I was at wit's end, I saw the captain stumbling out of the debris on the far side of the house. He was black as a chimney sweep, and had a red gash on his forehead. When he got closer,

I saw he was clutching my fur coat in one hand and Elizabeth's teddy bear in the other. I couldn't help bursting into tears.

We returned to the cellar as quickly as possible. I cleaned his wound with a wet cloth, and bandaged it with the rest of the gauze in my first-aid kit. I hoped this would suffice until he could reach a hospital or emergency station in the morning. When I finished, he seemed exhausted. He slumped down on the floor beside the others and slept soundly.

By this time, it was almost dawn. Although the flames had died down, I knew it was not yet time to move on. There was still a black pall over the city, and we would have great difficulty making our way. From the Hamburg raid I knew how long it took daylight to break through a city after an attack. As I remembered, it didn't get light until after ten o'clock. On the other hand, I didn't want to delay too long because I feared there would be another attack. In most cities that the R.A.F. worked over by night, the American Flying Fortresses finished the job around noon when the smoke had cleared well enough to see the target.

At the moment, there was nothing to do but wait. And each of us, alone with his thoughts and fears, sat or sprawled in the quiet cellar, waiting for the hours to pass. Several times I lit my candle to make sure the children were sleeping. I could see Hilda with her head slumped over, and the captain with his bandaged brow. His eyes were closed, but the blood was oozing through the gauze. Frau Bostel stared straight ahead with unseeing eyes, her bottle-blond hair disheveled. I could only guess at the extent of her despair. Every hour or so, I crept upstairs to watch for the coming of daylight. I longed to get underway—out of the burning city—and the waiting seemed endless.

Finally, shortly before ten, the heavy black smoke began to lift enough so that we could see our way. I awakened our group. The captain looked pale, but he insisted on helping me upstairs with the carriage. When we talked about the best way to get out of town, he surprised me by saying that he had decided to stay in Dresden. After all, it was his headquarters, he said. To leave would make him a deserter. "Besides," he asked, "where would I go?" I could see his point even though I felt it was better for everybody to get as far away from the city as possible. Reluctantly we said goodbye; I hated to have him leave us. But we gave him a dry blanket and some ration cards, which I hoped would be of use to him.

We had not planned to take Frau Bostel on our flight, but she begged to go with us. "I have no place to go," she sobbed. We knew her husband was at the front—and of course she had lost everything. Although I realized her blindness might slow us down to the danger point, I didn't see how we could leave her behind. "Come ahead," I said. "We'll manage."

As we started to walk, the smoke lifted a good deal, and there was considerable light. I was frantic to get out of the city before a daylight raid, and when I saw that there was no more danger from fire or sparks, we left our wet blankets behind. It made the going much easier.

The streets were empty, but what an eerie emptiness! The pale sun that broke through the darkened sky lit our route with a strange yellow-gray light. What had once been proud, solid homes were now smoking ruins—piles of meaningless stones, bricks, and charred beams. Almost every house was burned out, and not a soul was in sight. Where had everybody gone? Were they all dead or still crouching in cellars?

I had part of the answer as we neared the Grosse Garten. I saw rows of corpses lying in the paths and streets—men, women and children. The trees were festooned with bits of clothing, pieces of furniture, bodies, and parts of bodies. It was obvious that panic-stricken people had rushed from their burning houses into what they believed would be the greater safety of an open park. There they had met death from fire, asphyxiation, bombs, and flying debris. The water in the fountain basin still rippled peacefully in the pale sunlight. I thought of the children that only yesterday were sailing their boats there.

I had planned to take a short-cut through the Grosse Garten, but I knew I must spare the children as much of this as I could. Consequently, we skirted the park, going along side streets where iron fences and stone walls were still standing. It felt weird to walk along streets that had been so lively only a few hours before and now to find them completely dead. It was like walking along the bottom of a deserted crater or perhaps on some distant planet.

We trudged on for a long time until the houses began to thin out and we knew we were at the edge of the city. Soon we reached a dirt road that ran south. I had no map and only a vague idea of the area, but I knew we had to continue south if we were ever to reach Austria. I had talked with Hilda, and she agreed that our best chance for survival lay in getting to her mother's place. She had said she would take us only if we were bombed out, and we'd certainly met those conditions.

★ ★ ★

The nightmarish journey to Austria is chronicled in Wahle's memorable book, *Ordeal By Fire.*

★ ★ ★

Anne Wahle wrote during the third quarter of the twentieth century.

★
★
★

I LOVE WAR AND
RESPONSIBILITY AND
EXCITEMENT. PEACE IS
GOING TO BE HELL ON ME.

—GEN. GEORGE C. PATTON

BEYOND THE RIVER KWAI

Lt. Eric Lomax

Those of us who have seen the riveting war film, *The Bridge Over the River Kwai*, know how terrible the prisoners of war were treated during the building of the infamous Burma-Siam Railway. How could a survivor of that daily hell ever forgive what was done to him?

Eric Lomax certainly could not—and his nightmares never ended.

Until . . .

★ ★ ★

As my London-bound train clicked over the rails that fall afternoon in 1989, my eyes were transfixed by a newspaper photo of an elderly Japanese. This was the man I had searched for—the one who had brutally tortured me years before.

Back in 1942, I was a prisoner of war in a Japanese concentration camp. A twenty-three-year-old lieutenant in charge of the signal section of the 5th Field Regiment, Royal Artillery, I was captured with my unit at the fall of Singapore. Hundreds of thousands of British troops were herded into camps to starve, rot and die. Some of us worked as slave laborers on the infamous Burma-Siam Railway depicted in the film *The Bridge Over the River Kwai*. To get supplies to Burma, Japan decided to build a railroad across a forbidding range of spiky mountains, a route so terrible that British colonial engineers had rejected it. Working under the fierce tropical sun, we captives used picks, saws and axes to clear out bamboo and tropical hardwood day after day.

A group of us was sent to a prison camp where we assisted Japanese railroad mechanics and engineers doing repairs. We were famished for news of the outside world. Scrounging bits of silver paper, wire, aluminum, and wax, we assembled a small radio set on which we could receive *All India Radio* from New Delhi. The radio gave us word of Allied victories in the Solomon Islands and Guadalcanal. The boost to our morale was tremendous.

We took the radio to our next camp, on the river Kwai. Here in snake-infested surroundings, in oppressive humidity and heat, we turned to it for hope. I drew a map of the area, which I kept hidden in a bamboo tube. At night I turned to my Bible. Reading Job, I echoed his prayer: "I am full of confusion; therefore see thou mine affliction; for it increaseth" (Job 10:15–16).

In August 1943 our captors discovered our radio. Five of us suspects were forced to stand at attention for twelve hours. As we stood under the blazing sun with flies and insects feeding on our sweaty and itching skin, tongues swollen from thirst, I thought of Christ on the cross.

A squad of drunken guards began beating us one by one with heavy pickax shafts. We had to watch each forty-minute beating, hear bones crack, and see blood stain the earth. When it was my turn the first blow shot scorching pain through me. Hundreds of blows followed. I felt as if I were plunging into an abyss and saw tremendous flashes of light. Boots crunched my face into the gravel; I heard my arms snap, my teeth break. In utter despair I could only cry out, "Jesus!"

Four other men were similarly beaten. Two of them died, and their bodies were flung into a latrine trench. The rest of us were thrown into bamboo cages about five feet long and two and a half feet wide. I'm more than six feet tall, so I couldn't stretch out. Huddled and cramped, I held up my broken arms to prevent my weight from crushing the unset bones. Large red ants swarmed over me and I couldn't sweep them away.

The next day I was dragged into a room for interrogation. At a table sat a small, almost delicate, young man with jet-black hair and a wide mouth. Next to him hunched a large, muscular NCO with a shaved head. The smaller man, who appeared to be in charge, introduced himself as an interpreter in his investigation of "wide-spread anti-Japanese activities." As the NCO barked his accusations, the interpreter said my colleagues had made full confessions, that they knew about my part in using the radio and passing news on to others.

"Lomax, you will be killed whatever happens," he said. "It will be to your advantage in the time remaining to tell the whole truth. You know how we deal with prisoners when we wish to be unpleasant."

I began to hate them both. The interpreter's voice grated on and on, giving me no rest. Even at night I was awakened and pulled into the room by the interpreter. For eighteen hours a day I sat, balancing my broken arms on my thighs, forced to hear the same questions over and over.

In between grillings I lay in the cage in my own filth. Mosquitoes swarmed over me. In my nightly delirium, I heard biblical words: "Behold, I stand at the door, and knock: if any man hear my voice, and open the door, I will come in to him."

One morning I was taken into the room to see my railway map spread out on the table. A barrage of questions exploded: "Were you planning to escape? Name the others." The interpreter's frustration mounted as I remained silent.

I can't remember what happened next. My fellow prisoners said my head was shoved into a big water-filled tub again and again. What I remember was being forced to lie on my back, tied down to a bench.

"Lomax, you will tell me . . ." spoke the smaller Japanese. With each question, the NCO struck my stomach, chest and arms with a heavy tree limb. "Lomax, you will tell."

Then the NCO took a hose and pressed its full torrent into my nostrils and mouth, gagging me, filling my lungs and stomach. It was like drowning on dry land. When the hose was removed, the interpreter spoke into my ear while the NCO struck me. I had nothing to say. Again that shock of water rising inside me.

I don't know how long they alternated the beatings and half drownings. Eventually we were transported to another camp, where we were forced to sit in cells cross-legged every day for thirty-six days, awaiting court-martial. In November 1943 I was sentenced to five years imprisonment and began a living death, wasting away to a walking skeleton.

When I was at the point of death, they would take me to the POW "hospital," where I would regain consciousness. Then back to prison. Meanwhile, rumors began to spread. We heard the Nazis were nearly destroyed; Rangoon had been captured. In the summer of 1945 fellow prisoners whispered about a new type of bomb used on Japan. Then one day American B-29 bombers dropped food and medical packages. We were free!

But *I* was not. I continued suffering the emotional effects of my torture. I took up my life in England, got married, served in the military and the colonial service, but my nightmares never ended.

I frightened Patti, my wife, by awakening screaming. Or I withdrew in cold silence. Psychiatric evaluation showed I suffered from wartime trauma, a kind of prolonged battle stress. I could not forget the Japanese who had hurt me. I wanted to harm them, in particular, the hated interpreter with his mechanical voice, "Lomax, you will tell."

I followed the news from Japan, noting that two camp commanders had been hanged for their part in my fellow prisoners' murders. But there was no trace of my interpreter.

Finally, I reached a former British Army chaplain who had been in contact with former Japanese soldiers. He told me he had found the interpreter. His name was Nagase Takashi and he lived in the city of Kurashiki. He said Takashi had become active in charitable causes near Kanburi and had built a Buddhist temple of peace close to the railway as an atonement. I reacted with cold skepticism.

Then in October 1989, I renewed a friendship with a fellow POW, Jim Bradley, whom I visited in Midhurst, a village in Sussex. We had a pleasant time, and over breakfast, he gave me a photocopy of a recent article from the Japan *Times*, an English-language paper published in Tokyo.

It was a story about Nagase Takashi, including his photo. All the way back to London on the train I studied the clipping, the old rancor rising in me. The photo depicted a slight, unsmiling man in a dark collarless shirt. The text told how the ailing seventy-one-year-old had devoted his life to making up for the Japanese Army's treatment of prisoners. It said he suffered terrible flashbacks of torturing a British POW who was accused of possessing a map.

I dropped the paper in my lap. He remembered me. A sense of triumph filled me. Now I knew where he lived. I wanted to see if his remorse was genuine. I wanted to see his sorrow. Some people suggested I forgive and forget. They mentioned Christ on the cross forgiving his tormentors. But how could I forgive after what I had been through?

My hate festered. Then in July 1991 a friend gave me a small paperback by Nagase called *Crosses and Tigers,* translated into English. In telling his wartime activities, Nagase described my torture. He said he shuddered every time he recalled it. He expressed his remorse and felt he had been forgiven.

Never, I thought. Patti was indignant. With my permission she wrote Nagase, telling how I had suffered. "How can you feel 'forgiven,' Mr. Nagase, if this particular prisoner of war has not yet forgiven you?"

More than a week later a tissue-thin envelope from Japan arrived. "Your letter has beaten me down," Nagase wrote my wife, "reminding me of my dirty old days." Patti had sent him a photo of me and Nagase observed, "He looks a healthy and tender gentleman, though I am not able to see the inside of his mind. Please tell him to live long until I can see him."

Suddenly, as I read, my anger began to seep away. In its place rose compassion. I began to think the unthinkable: that I might meet Nagase face-to-face, without rancor.

My reply was brief and informal. It took a year to arrange our meeting. Patti and I flew to Bangkok and took a train to Kanburi, where Nagase and I would rendezvous at the old prison-camp site on the river Kwai.

On a hot, sunny day I stood on a terrace by the bridge, watching my former adversary walk toward me. I had forgotten how small he was, a tiny man in a straw hat, loose kimono-like jacket and trousers.

He began a formal bow, his creased face agitated. I took his hand and said in Japanese, "Good morning, Mr. Nagase. How are you?"

He looked up, trembling, with tears in his eyes. "I am very, very sorry," he said over and over.

I led him to the shade and we talked about our mutual experiences. It was obvious he had suffered much too. "I think I can die safely now," he said. As we walked around the area where the prison camp once stood, we discovered much in common: books, teaching, an interest in history. But still my words of forgiveness would not come.

Finally, back in Tokyo, when he and I were alone in a hotel room, I handed him a letter saying he had been most courageous in arguing against militarism and working for reconciliation. There I assured him of my total forgiveness.

Overcome with emotion, we spent some time talking quietly, two men now united. I felt peaceful and whole again. In the months to come, my nightmares seldom returned. When we forgive others, God blesses us.

Near the end of our visit in Japan, we two couples toured a museum in Hiroshima. Our wives walked ahead as Nagase and I talked about the last days of the war. He was astonished that we prisoners had heard about the nuclear attack on Hiroshima two days before he and his unit were told.

"How could you have known?" he asked. "You had no contact with the outside world."

"Ah," I said. "But we had another radio."

Together, we laughed.

★ ★ ★

Eric Lomax, a survivor of torture in a World War II prisoner-of-war camp, writes from his home in the United Kingdom.

★
★
★

| YOU CANNOT QUALIFY WAR IN

HARSHER TERMS THAN I WILL.

WAR IS CRUELTY, AND YOU

CANNOT REFINE IT.

—GEN. WILLIAM TECUMSEH SHERMAN

A NEW SKIPPER FOR CHARLIE COMPANY

KEN JONES

The Korean hill was scorched black from the firepower that left jagged wounds in the hill's crust. Jones observed to the colonel that taking "Old Hateful" must have been "quite a show."

The colonel answered, "Are you interested in the story—the *real* story?"

And this is the story he told: the story of a fine-looking Marine officer who felt unfit to lead his men into battle; unfit for a rather strange reason.

★ ★ ★

"We'd better keep pretty much on the move," said the colonel. "Every time I come up here the Reds seem to know it. I *always* draw enemy fire!"

We had traversed perhaps a mile or more of the trench system which delimits the Main Line of Resistance of the Korean battle-front, north and slightly west of Seoul. The traverse trenches were shallow in spots, and even when I scooched down, the top of my tin hat bobbed along above the parapet. The trench line was jagged, running up and down across the faces of endless rocky hills, and we had slid down and climbed up so much as we made our way painfully along that I was beginning to feel exhausted. Then we'd come, finally, to a small, flat piece of frozen ground about five yards square and at a good elevation, which allowed us to look down on the enemy positions immediately in front and perhaps a thousand yards away.

Between their lines and ours were a jumble of hills, a scattering of huge boulders, and a patch or two of scrub growth. The craggy shoulder of a cliff running upward and back into our positions par-tially screened the hard-stand where the colonel and I stood, and here we'd paused to uses our glasses. But experience had taught the colonel the danger of remaining too long in one spot, where the glint of the weak, winter sun on the lenses of his high-powered binoculars could betray his position to the enemy. Prudence prompted him to keep moving. There was, indeed, little to see save desolation. The muttering of artillery stumbled back and forth across the MLR in fitful waves, east to west and back again. There was the occasional chatter of a machine gun or recoilless rifle, some-times fairly close at hand, as often, at a remote distance. The pale, warmthless sun hung discouraged in the sky. It was the typical gray day of somber tones and shadows which heralds hardening weather north of "Thirty-eight."

Despite the colonel's warning, I found myself loath to break off my contemplation of a moderately tall, bulky, dome-topped hill which presented a fair eminence in the middle distance between the dug-in lines. Deep defiles scarred the face of the rise. But, while the shape and location of the hill made it apparent that it would be a dominant and key position in any attempt at mobile warfare in this area, the factor which held my attention was inescapable evidence that it *had* been just that. For the sides and top of this flinty hill were scorched—scorched black with searing, livid fire. Here and there was a jagged gash of raw earth and rock where a shell had opened a new wound beneath the carbonized crust left by flame-throwers, and grenades, and weapons of every conceivable sort and caliber. Although it slumbered now, even I could see that this position recently had been the site of a desperate, raging firefight, with no quarter asked or given. Security imposes constraints, so we'll call this hill "Old Hateful"—as good a name as any.

"That must have been quite a show," I observed to the colonel, as I reluctantly lowered my own glasses and followed him back into the trench system, headed for Battalion H.Q.

"More of a show than you think," he told me, as we turned a right angle in the trench and started scrambling up a sharp grade, clutching at any handhold that offered and generally making heavy weather of it. "Are you interested in the story—the *real* story?"

"Indeed I am," I assured him between gasps for breath.

"Well, it's not really mine to tell," he said thoughtfully. "It's the chaplain's story. I'll send him around."

That evening I sat in my tent back at Regiment working on my notes. The reports which I have made on the Korean war are not the products of press conferences held in comfortable quarters, nor yet of mimeographed handouts carefully prepared by sharp young lads in soldier suits. Whenever possible, I have tried to go to the scenes of action, make my own observations, and report accordingly. The United States Army, or at least its representatives in the Pentagon, is not too happy about such a forthright approach to its somewhat mixed-up war, and imposes limitations of time and restraints upon freedom of action which make a reporter's job both physically and technically difficult, and expose him to the possibility of error despite his best efforts.

I was mindful of all this as I worked away over the stained wads of paper on which I'd jotted precise notes under all sorts of conditions—riding in jeeps, sitting in bunkers, squatting in trenches, sitting out in the open at artillery emplacements. The bare electric bulb hanging down by the forward tentpole cast an uncertain, yellow illumination which failed to penetrate as far as the entrance to the sand-bagged "bug-out"—emergency shelter—which adjoined the rear of the large tent. Four field cots were ranged against the side walls, a rolled-up sleeping bag occupying the center of each. A shallow pan of water steamed lazily away on the oil stove near the front entrance, and the night was quiet save for the deep and distant rumble of artillery which served only to italicize the seeming tranquility of the locality. Somewhere around nine o'clock a light tap on the tentpole interrupted my preoccupation with my notes.

"Come!" I called.

The front of the tent parted and out of the night stepped a striking man. He was tall, white-haired, and he wore the insignia of a Marine Corps officer. (His rank, I learned later, was that of Lieutenant of the Navy, but serving with the Marines he wore the uniform of the Corps.)

"I'm Chaplain Morrison," he said, advancing with outstretched hand. (NOTE: For valid reasons I have been requested not to identify military personnel appearing in this report. The name Morrison is a pseudonym for a chaplain well known throughout the Navy, and having a record of gallant service with the United States Marines in the Korean war.) "You were interested in the story of Charlie Company?"

"They fought at 'Old Hateful?'" I inquired.

"They *captured* 'Old Hateful,'" he corrected me quietly. And then he sat down on a cot, and I pushed my work to one side—and this was the way of it, as the chaplain told me the story there in the cold Korean night:

★ ★ ★

Charlie Company was in reserve. As a unit they were a new outfit around here, although some of the men may well have been in battle before; I just don't know about that.

It was just after supper—a night about like this; maybe not so cold, but the stars were bright, I remember that well. I'd been stooging around, shooting the breeze here and there, and I was just about to peel off and leave. Matter of fact, I was approaching the chaplain's tent—funny; we always call it "the chaplain's tent," sort of like "the Auditorium," although I might just as well call it *my* tent—when I met Captain Jim. He was the skipper of Charlie Company, and a fine figure of a Marine officer he was—nearly six feet, one hundred eighty pounds, with regular features and dark hair. It was obvious that he'd been waiting for me.

"Hi, Jim," I greeted him. "What do you know for sure?"

"We've got our orders; we're moving up, Padre," he told me.

"Yes, I know, Jim. The Exec told me this afternoon. You're moving out in three days." I paused after that, because I wanted to appear casual. "Is there anything I can do?"

Captain Jim didn't answer right off. He looked out through the darkness, and I knew he was thinking—thinking *hard.*

"I don't know," he said at last. "I feel a great responsibility, Padre."

"You *have* a great responsibility, Jim," I told him.

"Militarily," he continued, seeming to take no notice of my reassurance, "militarily I'm not worried. I believe I know my job. But I'm beginning to realize that there's something more to it than that."

Again he fell silent and I waited. I've found from long experience that in times like this it's best to listen. Finally Jim spoke again, and now his voice, although still low and earnest, had a vibrant quality of urgency which seemed to add dimension to the little drama—for drama it was, although without histrionics.

"I haven't got a grip on the spiritual values," said Jim evenly. "And I know they're important; vitally important. Without that understanding I feel like a hypocrite, Padre. I can't urge my men to religious participation, which I know they need and need badly, when I myself do not participate. There's something missing in Charlie Company," he concluded with a heavy sigh. "Something of utmost importance."

Jim and I talked quietly for a while there in the darkness, and I learned something more of his problems. He was a young officer—scarcely thirty-two—and he sincerely wanted to be the leader his men needed. He was not worried about physical courage; that he had. But he knew that something more than physical courage was going to be needed for the ordeal ahead. He felt the need of more strength—not physical strength, but spiritual strength—to face his responsibilities.

"Maybe Charlie Company needs a new skipper," he said at last, and bitterly.

"You may be right, Jim," I told him. "And I've got a hunch there's a new skipper on the way for Charlie Company—but I don't think there'll be any call for changes in the Battalion records! Hit the sack now, and we'll go into this a little deeper in the morning."

During the next couple of days I worked with Captain Jim and the men of Charlie Company. They were all in about the same boat. Jim had neglected spiritual values all his life. Now, in the face of the heaviest responsibility a man can face—responsibility for the lives of his comrades and the honor of his organization—he woke up. He didn't have that conviction, that sureness, that inner tranquility which the challenge demanded.

The men of Charlie Company were average young Americans.

Most of them, as children, had had church affiliation of one sort or another. But religion and spiritual values had definitely been secondary until the blue chips went down. They didn't yet know the true nature of their need, but they were turning anxiously and questioningly to Captain Jim; he sensed their unrest, and he knew their need; he was striving desperately to fill it along with his own.

On the third day, early in the morning, Jim called me. "We'll saddle up about noon, Padre. I wish you'd conduct that 'going away' service you spoke of."

"I'll be there, Jim," I told him.

I found Jim and his men in the Company area. Their gear was piled all around—bed rolls, weapons, mess kits, tin hats—and they were waiting to mount the trucks. It was no time to be long-winded, so I kept it short. I had my field organ set up, and although the threat of storm hung oppressive in the air I announced a hymn, and the sober men of Charlie Company raised their voices in supplication and faith:

Lead on, O King eternal,
The day of march has come;
Henceforth in fields of conquest
Thy tents shall be our home:
Through days of preparation
Thy grace has made us strong,
And now, O King eternal
We lift our battle song.

They sang the *A-men*, the trucks rumbled out, and the storm broke.

The battle seasoning of Charlie Company was a rough business. The Company CP was under almost continuous artillery fire. Those whose duty permitted hid in the bunkers—even as you and

I!—and looked at each other with those flickering glances which speak plain of fear felt deep but denied. The enemy infiltrated between their positions and their supply sources. They took MIAs, and WIAs, and KIAs, and the nights were filled with terror and desperation. But they stuck it out; they held their positions; and they grew in spiritual strength—they and their skipper.

I took communion regularly to the men of Charlie Company as they faced a crafty enemy across a bleak and bitter terrain. In every bunker, three or four men would receive the sacrament, some for the first time, as the artillery and mortars pounded overhead and the earth shook loose in little cascades from the walls. Many of the men were embarrassed at first, but their need for strength and solace overcame their dim shame; they sank to their knees, closed their eyes, and bared their souls.

Word of my arrival would run ahead of me along Charlie Company's front, and as I entered each successive bunker men would ask hesitantly if they might partake of the sacrament: were they *good* enough? They were—and they *did*.

In one bunker—and could any man experiencing it ever forget it?—three men had moved everything off the top of the ammo box they were using for a table. They had a few candle ends—their only source of light. These they'd heated by holding them in their hands until the wax was soft. Then they'd stuck the pieces together to make one rickety candle perhaps six inches high. I started to protest, but I quickly realized that any protest would have been very wrong. That ammo box and that pieced-out candle were my altar—and who shall say that the gleaming altar cloth and towering taper of a cathedral found greater favor at the throne of God?

Well, when the test came Charlie Company was ready! One morning the enemy was observed powerfully established and dug in on "Old Hateful," the blackened hill you saw today. It was up to Charlie Company to toss 'em off.

I'm sure you could tell, just from the blackened shell that's left, how fierce the fighting was in, around, and on top of that hill. Charlie Company took casualties—*lots* of casualties. But they never showed the least sign of losing their grip. They surged to the top, were beaten off by merciless fire, and then they surged to the top again. They tossed grenades into the trenches and bunkers on the reverse slope; they fixed their bayonets and used 'em; they clung to every handhold and foothold—every crack and crevice—and in the end the enemy'd had enough.

Of course, Captain Jim was in the heart of all this fighting. He was, indeed, the "new" skipper of Charlie Company. I don't know whether you can understand it; maybe you can't unless you see and feel it. But he was a new man. He'd found those values which he knew he needed, and he'd helped his men to find them too.

★ ★ ★

The padre stood, buttoned his topcoat, turned up the collar, and took a step toward the tent opening. As he held out his hand to bid me good night he added:

"I don't imagine it was too hard for Charlie Company—finding the moral strength they needed, I mean. Because we people here in the front lines—we can see the finger of God moving here; *see it as never before!*"

I knew, because I'd seen it too.

★ ★ ★

Ken Jones wrote during the middle years of the twentieth century.

★
★   HE WHO COMMANDS THE
★
      SEA HAS COMMAND OF

      EVERYTHING.

              —THEMISTOCLES (ATHENIAN GENERAL)

MERCY
FLIGHT

LT. ALAN D. FREDERICKS
(WITH MICHAEL GLADYCH)

L t. Fredericks remembers like it was yesterday a night when
the motto of the 38th Air Rescue Squadron, "That Others
May Live," was put to the ultimate test. Did it really mean
to risk one's own life for some unknown person?

He was to find out.

★ ★ ★

I looked at the crew chief's face, ghostly white in the incandescent
light shafting through the half-open hangar door. He jerked his
thumb toward my SH-19 helicopter. "She's all set." The way he
spoke it, it sounded like, "It's your funeral."

Reaching for the step to climb into the cockpit, I slipped on the
icy concrete. The burning feeling in my stomach I'd had since the
Duty Officer got me out of bed ten minutes before, flared through
my body like an electric shock. I cursed.

The low, snow-pregnant clouds rolled fast, whipped by wind gusts. The weather report said, "Icing. Visibility down to zero. Snow showers." Here in Northern Japan "showers" was a camouflage word for blizzards that spewed sticky snow by the ton. I took a deep breath of the cold air. There was still time to back down.

Lieutenant Ed Brown, my copilot, leaned out of the cockpit window. "Well, what's the verdict?" he said with a forced chuckle. "That mess is below the healthy minimum. . . ."

I sensed he was giving me a way out, but I didn't take it. I climbed in and started the engine.

Staff Sergeant "Smokey" Collins, our paramedic, was already in the cabin in the back. As I let the engine warm up, I peered toward the large sign on the hangar. I couldn't read it, but I knew what it said by heart: "38th Air Rescue Squadron, Misawa Air Force Base." And on the bottom, in fancy Gothic script: "That others may live."

I pulled the worn, squadron joke. "That others may live it up," I said in the intercom; Ed didn't even give his usual snort.

At one minute past midnight, I threw in the rotor clutch. The blades picked up speed and started their hysterical pitch. . . . We were off.

We were still in a hover when a gust of wind kicked the chopper up like a plastic toy, then slammed it down. Momentarily, the rotor blades flapped as though in a vacuum. The chopper rattled and shook, falling out of control. I braced myself for a crash, but the rotor bit into an uplift, halting the crazy dive a foot off the ground. I should have cut the power and landed, but I was paralyzed and a split second later another gust sucked us away and into the dark sky.

My innards were still twisted in a knot when the air smoothed out. I was glad I hadn't landed. Nobody likes to chicken out, especially in a Rescue outfit. Well, I thought, the mission was short—forty miles to the Ominato radar site. A few minutes to slide that poor kid with the hot appendix into the cabin. . . . We should be back in Misawa in about an hour. . . .

At eight hundred feet now, brushing against the cloud bellies, ahead and to my right, I could see the lights of villages scattered on the snow-covered countryside. I set course for Kikusabashi, a small village on the Matsu Bay shore, and relaxed. Once we get to the bay, I figured, I'll turn and follow the coastline all the way to Ominato. Even if we do get a blizzard or two, I'll be able to fly low and keep an eye on the narrow beach. No sweat.

The cockpit heater pumped a comforting warmth and that tightness in the pit of my stomach melted away. Then, without warning, the first shower hit.

Wet snow plastered the windshield and froze the wipers solid. In a second, the cockpit turned into a giant fish bowl with the grotesque reflections of the luminous dials jeering at me from the curved plexiglass panes.

I tensed as I focused on the instrument panel. It doesn't take much to lose eight hundred feet of altitude and get smeared into a bloody suki-yaki over the ground, especially with the hopper weighted by snow. So I watched the altimeter as never before. The blizzard is too rough to last long, I kept telling myself. We'll be out of the mess soon.

The gauges read steady—straight and level. The snow outside reflected the navigation lights back into the cockpit and lit up the instrument panel like a neon sign—red and green flashing in turn. Soon, I caught myself moving my head from side to side with each flash—red—green—red—green.

Suddenly, I felt as though the chopper had tilted and I was falling out of my seat. The pitch of the rotor blades knifing through the blizzard rose to a scream. We were slipping—we were going to crash! I yanked the stick to level off and felt the chopper respond with a shudder. Then I saw the artificial horizon tilt and I froze in horror.

What I had felt to be a slip was the deadly vertigo. The chopper had been level all the time, but having given in to the hypnotic confusion, and trying to recover from the illusory slip, I was now plunging at sixty knots toward the ground. My heart pounded in my throat. My hand tightened on the stick as I wrestled with myself to bring the chopper back to level. It felt like jumping from a sixtieth-floor window to save yourself from death by fire. I *knew* I had to center the stick—trust instruments or die. Yet, every fiber of my body screamed that the *#?+ instruments were wrong.

The altimeter unwound . . . 500 feet . . . 300 . . . 100 . . . 50 . . . With a last, frantic effort I forced my hand to obey and revved up the engine. The altimeter touched Zero, quivered and started to climb again.

★ ★ ★

My first thought was to turn back and land at Misawa. But if I did, I would still have to fly through this storm, which would probably beat me back to the field anyway. Now, flying into the wind—I'd be out of this mess sooner.

I remembered my flight instructor's words: "You know what happens to a pilot who goes to Hell? He has eternal vertigo." I laughed at it then, but now I lived the insane torture, a maddening seesaw of reason and instinct, like those miserable navigation lights flashing red and green.

Those monotonous flashes made me sick to my stomach. Who needed navigation lights in this soup anyway? I slipped the switch off and a miracle happened. As suddenly as it had come, my vertigo confusion vanished. It must have been the flashing that hypnotized me and almost scored another vertigo victim.

Columbus couldn't have been happier than I was over my discovery. I laughed aloud, but I laughed too soon. Worn out by the struggle, my right hand now trembled, losing its grip on the stick.

And letting go of controls in the SH-19 is sure-fire suicide. "Take over, Ed!" I yelled to Brown.

He did. A moment later, we popped out of the storm, the windshield wipers picked up again and I could see the Hiku-sabashi lights on the Matsu Bay shore dead ahead. How I had managed to hold a straight course, I didn't know and didn't care. I slumped back in my seat, happy to be alive and wishing I were home in Kearney, Nebraska.

The sharp contrast of the snowed-under beach and the dark sea made a perfect line to follow. From now on, we would have to stick to that line like a train to its tracks. And no matter how bad the visibility, from now on we could no longer fly instruments because a little inland, to our right, there was a cliff and rugged hills we could easily pile into.

By the time Ed made the turn, my hand felt rested and I took the controls again. I poured on the coal and watched the surf. In about 10 minutes we would hit the halfway mark at Hamada—a small village on the coast.

I flipped on the intercom. "Keep your eyes glued to that coastline, Ed."

He had no time to acknowledge, for another blizzard sneaked up on us. After the first thick flurry, the snow let up, the wipers worked fine and I could make out the beach all right. But gradually, I was forced to slow down as the snow began to blot out the surf— our lifeline.

After a few minutes, even at our turtle pace and staring glassy-eyed, I was losing the coastline. I got closer to the deck, skimming over the surf; but now the wind got gusty and threatened to smash us against the cliff. My hand started to tremble on the stick and my legs, tired from parrying the gusts, jerked a wild tattoo on the pedals. To make things worse, the wipers slowed down under the weight of the piling snow.

I had only one way out. I slowly veered left—over the open water. Maybe I could bypass the blizzard, I figured. But instead of abating, the snow got even thicker. A few feet off the angry breakers, I flew the chopper mostly by feel, getting an occasional glimpse of the water below through the wide window.

★ ★ ★

We couldn't go on. I slowed down to a hover, trying to figure out my next move. I had to land before we got blown against the hills. The point was—where? The beach was too narrow. Still, maybe I'll find a spot wide enough, I thought. Sweating out the precarious altitude and praying for the wipers to keep working, I crept back toward the shore.

The wipers gave a scraping groan and froze solid. We've had it, I said to myself, feeling that old knot squeezing my stomach. A gust of wind squashed the chopper down. We hit! Instinctively, I yanked back on the stick. We still flew. The spray washed the snow off the windshield and there, ahead, I thought I saw a weak blotch of light.

Must be vertigo again, or something, I thought. But Ed's voice came through the intercom. "Do you see what I see?" he stammered.

If Ed saw it too, the light must have been real. "Watch that light, Ed. For Pete's sake, don't lose it."

Like a moth attracted by flame, I headed into the light. When the snow plastered the windshield, I swerved the chopper right and left, each time getting a glimpse of our life-saving beacon.

We made it! It was a warehouse with a large, flood-lit parking area on the cliff. As I hovered a few feet off the ground, my rotor kicked up a snow storm of its own. But, blind or not, I was going to set that chopper down.

The landing gear took a sickening wallop and I switched off. In the few seconds it took the rotor to stop milling, the snow thickened, blacking out even the strong lights only a few feet away. Had we been one minute later getting to the spot, we would have missed the lights and smashed for sure into those hills.

★ ★ ★

I leaned back and panted like a pug after a fifteen-round bout. Smokey poked his head in from the cabin. "Where's the patient, Lieutenant?" the paramedic said.

"At Ominato. This is Hamada—at least, that's what we figure."

It was 1 a.m. We were due back at Misawa with the sick man. If the Duty Officer didn't hear from us, he would push the panic button and another crew would stick their necks out to search for us. For that reason, and to check the Ominato weather, we tried to raise Misawa on our radio. The command-set static crackled like the blooming thing was going to blow up. The UHF radio was no good—we were too far and too low. We tried Ominato—again, no soap.

"What do we do now?" Ed said. "Send a carrier pigeon?"

"There's bound to be a phone somewhere," I said. "Maybe in that warehouse."

Smokey and Ed immediately volunteered to go. But I pulled my rank on them. After all, I was the aircraft commander and it was my job. If I found that the weather at Ominato was good, we would wait for the storm to let up and take off.

I climbed out, slipped on the step and fell, getting dunked in the snowdrift. After the warm cockpit, it was like diving into the Bering Sea. I struggled up, plodded to the warehouse, and tried the doors; but they were locked tight, with no sign of life anywhere.

I did find a telephone lead from the warehouse, followed it and located a pole. My teeth chattering, wishing I had stayed put in the warm cockpit, I headed into the blizzard—groping from one pole to the next. There had to be a house somewhere. . . .

An icy crust formed on my flight overalls and the wind beat the wet snow into my face. I stopped at every pole, turned my back to the gale to catch a breath; then I pushed on to the next stop.

The whole thing didn't make sense, I thought, gasping. Rescue or not, a guy has to draw a line somewhere. Why do I knock myself out for one sick airman? So I'm yellow—so what? I turned back, lost my footing and sprawled into the snow.

I lay in some kind of hollow. Blood pounded in my head like a trip hammer. Sheltered from the wind I felt warm and comfortable. . . . I needed a breather. I figured I would rest for ten minutes. I scraped the ice from my wrist watch—I'd been walking for half an hour. Half an hour? I must have come close to the village. . . .

One part of my brain was telling me to relax and stay in the hollow. But the other part hollered to keep moving. It was like somebody standing over me, shouting, "Get up and walk." But how was I supposed to when I couldn't even move my legs! To prove it to myself, I tried to bend my left leg and a cramp jabbed at my calf muscles like a branding iron. The pain sobered me. As I rubbed my aching leg, I started to think clearly.

You'll die of exposure, you dope, I told myself. Get up and move!

Fighting the cramp, I crawled out and staggered on. A wind eddy momentarily blew the snow away and there, a few paces ahead was a dark mass of a house.

No lights showed, but I could make out a telephone line leading to the place. I found the door, and pounded on it with my fists.

The door opened and I fell into the light and warmth. When I wiped the snow off my eyes, I saw a Japanese farmer standing over me, gaping as if he'd seen a ghost.

I couldn't make my mouth work, which was just as well. I didn't know much Japanese anyway. But as I dragged myself to my feet, I made signs. The guy caught on. "*Denwá, hai, hai . . .*" he said, leading the way to the telephone.

I had some trouble trying to get the operator to put me through to Misawa, but after a few minutes I heard an American voice. Then I got the Duty Officer.

He said the blizzards evidently bypassed Ominato and the weather there was okay. I told him I would try taking off as soon as visibility permitted. Then, thanking the Japanese in sign language, I started back.

It wasn't so bad now with the wind pushing me. Also, the storm was abating. I could now see the warehouse lights from way off. And by the time Ed hoisted me into the cockpit and I thawed out, we could see far enough to start up the windmill.

We made it to Ominato with no more sweat. In only moments, the patient was carried on board, in Smokey's care. The sick kid, Airman 2nd Class Francis E. Laws, was well doped up, Smokey reported, and he ought to make it all right.

I'd wanted to fly the chopper back. "I've just been talking to Misawa," he told me. "They expect the weather to stay clear there for another hour. Why don't you take a rest?"

My hands still trembled and I was shivering in my wet clothes like an engine missing on half the cylinders. But I wasn't going to miss the easy part of the trip, so we shoved off with me at the controls.

I barreled along the coast at top speed. I wasn't taking any chances on that weather forecast. Suddenly, the chopper bucked and sideswept as if an oversized mule had kicked it in the tail rotor, and my head banged against the window. Recovering, I chopped the power fast.

Flying a helicopter in rough air is like walking a tightrope. If you fly too fast, you might lose the rotor and, before you can say "collective pitch control," you're the subject of a brief obituary in the base newspaper. But if you slow down too much, you risk getting rotor blade-tip stall and falling out of the sky. It's not much of a choice, especially flying ten feet off the water.

★ ★ ★

Like a fighter with both eyes pummeled blind, I tried to outguess the invisible hooks and jabs, but all I could do was to take the beating and pray that the next gust wouldn't be the K.O. punch.

I no longer shivered. Sweat mixed with melting ice trickled down my back and burned in my eyes. My hands were clammy. I had to wipe them off. "Ed! Take . . ."

A tip stall stopped us with a powerful uppercut under the chopper's chin. The machine pointed its snout into the low clouds, shook and buffeted as though it were going to fall apart. The jolt slammed me against my seat belt and knocked off my headset. The beach, the breakers, crazily pulled from under us like a trap-door.

Hanging in the air, tail down, we had to crash. That sickening knowledge stretched split-seconds into deathly infinity. There was that roller-coaster emptiness in my stomach as we started down. Between my hammering pulse beats I desperately juggled the throttle . . . the pitch. . . . Then the chopper responded. We were level now, but falling like a ton of bricks. The rotor blades strained. A shiver ran through the fuselage. I tensed.

The landing gear smashed into a whitecap. Spray lashed the windshield. I pulled back on the stick. A merciful gust helped us up. We were still flying.

As soon as Ed found my headset I checked with Smokey. "Is the patient okay?"

"Yes, sir. Strapped down tight."

"The chopper can't take this much longer. We've got to land again. Will the kid hold out?"

"Hope we don't have to stay down long. His heart doesn't sound so good."

Knowing you've got to land is one thing and finding a landing place at night is another—especially since it had started to snow again. If only we could make it to Hamada. . . .

Ed spotted the light to our left. Thinking it was the old warehouse, I headed for it, the snow getting thicker. I had a choice—speed up and risk losing the rotor in the gusts or take it slow and lose the light. I remembered how fast the blizzard blacked out the light at Hamada. My hands and feet twitched and I didn't know how long I could keep flying in this mess. I took a chance and plowed toward that light.

I aimed close to the blurring lights and eased the chopper down by feel. This time, too, the blizzard picked up as soon as we touched down. We kept the engine idling to run the cabin heater and I stretched in my seat, soaking up the relaxing warmth.

After awhile, Smokey called from the cabin. "The kid's heart beat is kind of peculiar. Could you try taking off, sir?"

I wiped the steam off the window. It was snowing to beat the band and the gusts rocked the chopper. "Can't do it, Smokey. We've got to sweat it out."

As soon as the blizzard abated, I crawled out to scrape the snow and ice off the windshield. The sky was turning gray and the place didn't look a bit like the Hamada warehouse. I swivelled my neck to case the situation and when I saw where we had landed I almost fainted.

We had squeezed into a midget rice paddy close to an electric power station. The main rotor tips cleared the high tension lines by inches on both sides. And as for the tail rotor—you could hardly put a hand between the blades and the branches of tall fir trees that surrounded it. We were trapped. And to cinch it, the rotor hub was bearded with foot-long icicles and the fuselage, weighted with iced-up snow, looked like Moby Dick.

Ed climbed out after me and his face paled. "Brother, let nobody tell me miracles don't happen," he said. "By the way, you're not thinking of flying this bird out of here?"

"Not me."

The only sensible thing to do was to call Misawa and ask them to send an ambulance. We still couldn't make radio contact since I had informed Operations I was going to land, but Ed suggested finding a telephone again. I was all set to let him go out when Smokey reached the cabin and tugged my leg.

"The sedative is wearing off," he said. "I can't risk giving the patient another shot. He's in bad shape, Lieutenant. You've got to get him to the hospital."

Even if the ambulance could get through the snow, it would take hours. If we were going to save the airman's life I had to make the insane decision to take off from that trap. I didn't recognize my voice when I said, "Come on, Ed. Let's get the egg beater off its frozen backside."

"There's one chance in a million we can make it," Ed said.

"I know, but we've got to try."

★ ★ ★

This was like trying to lift a piece out of the middle of a jigsaw puzzle without upsetting the picture. And what a cotton-picking upset it would make! The slightest wrong move could wreck our tail rotor, and with that little fan gone, nothing would stop us from making high-voltage fireworks. We'd fry in this chopper alive.

What a confounded irony, I thought. A few hours ago I was praying for a place to land. Well, I'd landed. And now I was praying again to take off in one piece. . . .

I rubbed my hands until they tingled. I scraped every bit of snow off my boots, lest my foot might slip on the pedal. The engine checked out all right. I breathed deeply and engaged the rotor clutch. The blades started to mill slowly. So far, so good. Then, the rotor revved up. The down-wash whipped the snow that hid the power lines from sight.

There was still time to quit, call for an ambulance and sweat it out. Ed knew it, too. "One chance in a million," he said again.

I throttled back. What chance did that kid have to live if we *did* wait. Smokey called from the cabin. "Anything wrong?"

"No. How's the kid?"

"Bad."

I took another deep breath and revved up the engine again. The chopper wobbled, shaking off the whirling snow. My belly tightened and my heartbeat seemed to pound over the engine's roar.

Something scraped in the back. Was it ice falling off or the tail rotor . . . those miserable trees . . . I froze at the controls. Another scratch. Something was letting go. The chopper shook and the vibration felt like a high-voltage current going through my body. High voltage! If I had busted that tail rotor. . . . Dear Lord!

The chopper gave an upward lurch. We shot out of the snow eddies. We were in the clear! I exhaled and a wooly weakness swept over me. How I kept flying I didn't know, but fifteen minutes later we landed in front of our hangar—the spot we had left over five hours before.

The corpsmen slid our patient out and as the ambulance rushed off to the hospital, the mechanics surrounded our chopper as though it were a sideshow freak.

The crew chief shook his head. "Now I've seen everything. If I hadn't watched you fly this iceberg in, I wouldn't have believed it could get off the ground!"

I was too shaky and tired to talk. But Smokey Collins patted the mechanic on the shoulder. "Buster," he said quietly, "you ain't seen nothing."

★ ★ ★

Alan Fredericks and Michael Gladyn wrote during the second half of the twentieth century.

★
★   A WAR, EVEN THE MOST
★   VICTORIOUS, IS A NATIONAL

MISFORTUNE.

—GEN. HELMUTH VON MOLTKE

MIKE'S FLAG

COMMANDER JOHN MCCAIN
(WITH MARK SALTER)

Over the years I've discovered that a story's power has nothing to do with its length. When a dear friend of ours (a Vietnam veteran) heard about this story collection, he had one request: track down this story. He said that he'd not been able to get through it yet without crying.

★ ★ ★

For well over five years, captured American aviators had been living through a daily hell of mistreatment, incarceration (much of it solitary confinement), and torture—all intended to break their spirit so that they would betray their country.

But they failed, maintains John McCain, who endured prison camps for over five interminable years. In his bestselling book, *Faith of My Fathers*, he shared this story.

★ ★ ★

Every POW knew that the harder the war was fought the sooner we would go home. Long aware of the on-and-off peace negotiations in Paris, we were elated when the Nixon administration proved it was intent on forcing the negotiations to a conclusion that would restore our freedom.

As the bombing campaign intensified, our morale soared with every sortie. It was after one raid, and our raucous celebration of its effect, that the guards dragged Mike Christian from our room.

Mike was a Navy bombardier-navigator who had been shot down in 1967, about six months before I arrived. He had grown up near Selma, Alabama. His family was poor. He had not worn shoes until he was thirteen years old. Character was their wealth. They were good, righteous people, and they raised Mike to be hardworking and loyal. He was seventeen when he enlisted in the Navy. As a young sailor, he showed promise as a leader and impressed his superiors enough to be offered a commission.

What packages we were allowed to receive from our families often contained handkerchiefs, scarves, and other clothing items. For some time, Mike had been taking little scraps of red and white cloth, and with a needle he had fashioned from a piece of bamboo, he laboriously sewed an American flag onto the inside of his blue prisoner's shirt. Every afternoon, before we ate our soup, we would hang Mike's flag on the wall of our cell and together recite the Pledge of Allegiance. No other event of the day had as much meaning to us.

The guards discovered Mike's flag one afternoon during a routine inspection and confiscated it. They returned that evening and took Mike outside. For our benefit as much as Mike's, they beat him severely, just outside our cell, puncturing his eardrum and breaking several of his ribs. When they had finished, they dragged him bleeding and nearly senseless back into our cell, and we helped him crawl to his place on the sleeping platform.

After things quieted down, we all lay down to go to sleep. Before drifting off, I happened to look toward a corner of the room, where one of the four naked lightbulbs that were always illuminated in our cell cast a dim light on Mike Christian. He had crawled there quietly when he thought the rest of us were sleeping. With his eyes nearly swollen shut from the beating, he had quietly picked up his needle and thread . . . and begun sewing a new flag.

★ ★ ★

John McCain, U.S. Senator from Arizona, lives and writes from his Arizona and Washington, D.C. homes. All of his books have become best-sellers.

★
★
★

TO BE PREPARED FOR WAR IS
ONE OF THE MOST EFFECTUAL
MEANS OF PRESERVING PEACE.

—GEORGE WASHINGTON

TAKING CHANCE

Lt. Col. Michael Strobl

C hance Phelps was wearing his Saint Christopher medal when he was killed on Good Friday. Eight days later, I handed the medallion to his mother. I didn't know Chance before he died. Today, I miss him.

★ ★ ★

Over a year ago, I volunteered to escort the remains of Marines killed in Iraq should the need arise. The military provides a uniformed escort for all casualties to ensure they are delivered safely to the next of kin and are treated with dignity and respect along the way.

Thankfully, I hadn't been called on to be an escort since Operation Iraqi Freedom began. The first few weeks of April, however, had been tough for the Marines. On the Monday after Easter I was reviewing Department of Defense press releases when I saw that a Private First Class Chance Phelps was killed in action outside of

Baghdad. The press release listed his hometown—the same town I'm from. I notified our Battalion adjutant and told him that, should the duty to escort PFC Phelps fall to our Battalion, I would take him.

I didn't hear back the rest of Monday and all day Tuesday until 1800. The Battalion duty NCO called my cell phone and said I needed to be ready to leave for Dover Air Force Base at 1900 in order to escort the remains of PFC Phelps.

Before leaving for Dover I called the major who had the task of informing Phelps's parents of his death. The major said the funeral was going to be in Dubois, Wyoming. (It turned out that PFC Phelps only lived in my hometown for his senior year of high school.) I had never been to Wyoming and had never heard of Dubois.

With two other escorts from Quantico, I got to Dover AFB at 2330 on Tuesday night. First thing on Wednesday we reported to the mortuary at the base. In the escort lounge there were about half a dozen Army soldiers and about an equal number of Marines waiting to meet up with "their" remains for departure. PFC Phelps was not ready, however, and I was told to come back on Thursday. Now, at Dover with nothing to do and a solemn mission ahead, I began to get depressed.

I was wondering about Chance Phelps. I didn't know anything about him; not even what he looked like. I wondered about his family and what it would be like to meet them. I did pushups in my room until I couldn't do any more.

On Thursday morning I reported back to the mortuary. This time there was a new group of Army escorts and a couple of the Marines who had been there Wednesday. There was also an Air Force captain there to escort his brother home to San Diego.

We received a brief covering our duties, the proper handling of the remains, the procedures for draping a flag over a casket, and of course, the paperwork attendant to our task. We were shown pictures of the shipping container and told that each one contained, in addition to the casket, a flag. I was given an extra flag since Phelps's parents were divorced. This way they would each get one. I didn't like the idea of stuffing the flag into my luggage but I couldn't see carrying a large flag, folded for presentation to the next of kin, through an airport while in my Alpha uniform. It barely fit into my suitcase.

It turned out that I was the last escort to leave on Thursday. This meant that I repeatedly got to participate in the small ceremonies that mark all departures from the Dover AFB mortuary.

Most of the remains are taken from Dover AFB by hearse to the airport in Philadelphia for air transport to their final destination. When the remains of a service member are loaded onto a hearse and ready to leave the Dover mortuary, there is an announcement made over the building's intercom system. With the announcement, all service members working at the mortuary, regardless of service branch, stop work and form up along the driveway to render a slow ceremonial salute as the hearse departs. Escorts also participate in each formation until it is their time to leave.

On this day there were some civilian workers doing construction on the mortuary grounds. As each hearse passed, they would stop working and place their hard hats over their hearts. This was my first sign that my mission with PFC Phelps was larger than the Marine Corps and that his family and friends were not grieving alone.

Eventually I was the last escort remaining in the lounge. The Marine Master Gunnery Sergeant in charge of the Marine liaison there came to see me. He had Chance Phelps's personal effects. He removed each item: a large watch, a wooden cross with a lanyard, two loose dog tags, two dog tags on a chain, and a Saint Christopher medal on a silver chain. Although we had been briefed that we might be carrying some personal effects of the deceased, this set me aback. Holding his personal effects, I was starting to get to know Chance Phelps.

Finally we were ready. I grabbed my bags and went outside. I was somewhat startled when I saw the shipping container, loaded three-quarters of the way into the back of a black Chevy Suburban that had been modified to carry such cargo. This was the first time I saw my "cargo" and I was surprised at how large the shipping container was. The Master Gunnery Sergeant and I verified that the name on the container was Phelps's, then they pushed him the rest of the way in and we left. Now it was PFC Chance Phelps's turn to receive the military—and construction workers'—honors. He was finally moving towards home.

As I chatted with the driver on the hour-long trip to Philadelphia, it became clear that he considered it an honor to be able to contribute in getting Chance home. He offered his sympathy to the family. I was glad to finally be moving yet apprehensive about what things would be like at the airport. I didn't want this package to be treated like ordinary cargo, but I knew that the simple logistics of moving around a box this large would have to overrule my preferences.

When we got to the Northwest Airlines cargo terminal at the Philadelphia airport, the cargo handler and hearse driver pulled the shipping container onto a loading bay while I stood to the side and executed a slow salute. Once Chance was safely in the cargo area, and I was satisfied that he would be treated with due care and respect, the hearse driver drove me over to the passenger terminal and dropped me off.

As I walked up to the ticketing counter in my uniform, a Northwest employee started to ask me if I knew how to use the automated boarding-pass dispenser. Before she could finish, another ticketing agent interrupted her. He told me to go straight to the counter, then explained to the woman that I was a military escort. She seemed embarrassed. The woman behind the counter already had tears in her eyes as I was pulling out my government travel voucher. She struggled to find words but managed to express her sympathy for the family and thank me for my service. She upgraded my ticket to first class.

After clearing security, I was met by another Northwest Airline employee at the gate. She told me a representative from cargo would be up to take me down to the tarmac to observe the movement and loading of PFC Phelps. I hadn't really told any of them what my mission was but they all knew.

When the man from the cargo crew met me, he, too, struggled for words. On the tarmac, he told me stories of his childhood as a military brat and repeatedly told me that he was sorry for my loss. I was starting to understand that, even here in Philadelphia, far away from Chance's hometown, people were mourning with his family.

On the tarmac, the cargo crew was silent except for occasional instructions to each other. I stood to the side and saluted as the conveyor moved Chance to the aircraft. I was relieved when he was finally settled into place. The rest of the bags were loaded and I watched them shut the cargo-bay door before heading back up to board the aircraft.

One of the pilots had taken my carry-on bag himself and had it stored near the cockpit door so he could watch it while I was on the tarmac. As I boarded the plane, I could tell immediately that the flight attendants had already been informed of my mission. They seemed a little choked up as they led me to my seat.

About forty-five minutes into our flight, I still hadn't spoken to anyone except to tell the first-class flight attendant that I would prefer water. I was surprised when the flight attendant from the back of the plane suddenly appeared and leaned down to grab my hands. She said, "I want you to have this" as she pushed a small gold crucifix, with a relief of Jesus, into my hand. It was her lapel pin and it looked somewhat worn. I suspected it had been hers for quite some time. That was the only thing she said to me the entire flight

When we landed in Minneapolis, I was the first one off the plane. The pilot himself escorted me straight down the side stairs of the exit tunnel to the tarmac. The cargo crew there already knew what was on this plane. They were unloading some of the luggage when an Army sergeant, a fellow escort who had left Dover earlier that day, appeared next to me. His "cargo" was going to be loaded onto my plane for its continuing leg. We stood side-by-side in the dark and executed a slow salute as Chance was removed from the plane. The cargo crew at Minneapolis kept Phelps's shipping case separate from all the other luggage as they waited to take us to the cargo area. I waited with the soldier and we saluted together as his fallen comrade was loaded onto the plane.

My trip with Chance was going to be somewhat unusual in that we were going to have an overnight stopover. We had a late start out of Dover and there was just too much traveling ahead of us to continue on that day. (We still had a flight from Minneapolis to Billings, Montana. Then a five-hour drive to the funeral home. That was to be followed by a ninety-minute drive to Chance's hometown.)

I was concerned about leaving him overnight in the Minneapolis cargo area. My ten-minute ride from the tarmac to the cargo holding area eased my apprehension. Just as in Philadelphia, the cargo guys in Minneapolis were extremely respectful and seemed honored to do their part. While talking with them, I learned that the cargo supervisor for Northwest Airlines at the Minneapolis airport is a Lieutenant Colonel in the Marine Corps Reserves. They called him for me and let me talk to him.

Once I was satisfied that all would be okay for the night, I asked one of the cargo crew if he would take me back to the terminal so that I could catch my hotel's shuttle. Instead, he drove me straight to the hotel himself. At the hotel, the lieutenant colonel called me and said he would personally pick me up in the morning and bring me back to the cargo area.

Before leaving the airport, I had told the cargo crew that I wanted to come back to the cargo area in the morning rather than go straight to the passenger terminal. I felt bad for leaving Chance overnight and wanted to see the shipping container where I had left it for the night. It was fine.

The lieutenant colonel made a few phone calls then drove me around to the passenger terminal. I was met again by a man from the cargo crew and escorted down to the tarmac. The pilot of the plane joined me as I waited for them to bring Chance from the cargo area. The pilot and I talked of his service in the Air Force and how he missed it.

I saluted as Chance was moved up the conveyor and onto the plane. It was to be a while before the luggage was to be loaded, so the pilot took me up to board the plane where I could watch the tarmac from a window. With no other passengers yet on board, I talked with the flight attendants and one of the cargo guys. He had been in the Navy and one of the attendants had been in the Air Force. Everywhere I went, people were continuing to tell me their relationship to the military. After all the baggage was aboard, I went back down to the tarmac, inspected the cargo bay, and watched them secure the door.

When we arrived at Billings, I was again the first off the plane. This time Chance's shipping container was the first item out of the cargo hold. The funeral director had driven five hours up from Riverton, Wyoming to meet us. He shook my hand as if I had personally lost a brother.

We moved Chance to a secluded cargo area. Now it was time for me to remove the shipping container and drape the flag over the casket. I had predicted that this would choke me up but I found I was more concerned with proper flag etiquette than the solemnity of the moment. Once the flag was in place, I stood by and saluted as Chance was loaded onto the van from the funeral home. I was thankful that we were in a small airport and the event seemed to go mostly unnoticed. I picked up my rental car and followed Chance for five hours until we reached Riverton. During the long trip I imagined how my meeting with Chance's parents would go. I was very nervous about that.

When we finally arrived at the funeral home, I had my first face-to-face meeting with the Casualty Assistance Call Officer. It had been his duty to inform the family of Chance's death. He was on the Inspector/Instructor staff of an infantry company in Salt Lake City, Utah and I knew he had had a difficult week.

Inside, I gave the funeral director some of the paperwork from Dover and discussed the plan for the next day. The service was to be at 1400 in the high school gymnasium up in Dubois, population about nine hundred, some ninety miles away. Eventually, we had covered everything. The CACO had some items that the family wanted to be inserted into the casket and I felt I needed to inspect Chance's uniform to ensure everything was proper. Although it was going to be a closed-casket funeral, I still wanted to ensure his uniform was squared away.

Earlier in the day I wasn't sure how I'd handle this moment. Suddenly, the casket was open and I got my first look at Chance Phelps. His uniform was immaculate—a tribute to the professionalism of the Marines at Dover. I noticed that he wore six ribbons over his marksmanship badge; the senior one was his Purple Heart. I had been in the Corps for over seventeen years, including a combat tour, and was wearing eight ribbons. This Private First Class, with less than a year in the Corps, had already earned six.

The next morning, I wore my dress blues and followed the hearse for the trip up to Dubois. This was the most difficult leg of our trip for me. I was bracing for the moment when I would meet his parents and hoping I would find the right words as I presented them with Chance's personal effects.

We got to the high school gym about four hours before the service was to begin. The gym floor was covered with folding chairs neatly lined in rows. There were a few townspeople making final preparations when I stood next to the hearse and saluted as Chance was moved out of the hearse. The sight of a flag-draped coffin was overwhelming to some of the ladies.

We moved Chance into the gym to the place of honor. A Marine sergeant, the command representative from Chance's battalion, met me at the gym. His eyes were watery as he relieved me of watching Chance so that I could go eat lunch and find my hotel.

At the restaurant, the table had a flier announcing Chance's service: Dubois High School gym; two o'clock. It also said that the family would be accepting donations so that they could buy flak vests to send to troops in Iraq.

I drove back to the gym at a quarter after one. I could've walked—you could walk to just about anywhere in Dubois in ten minutes. I had planned to find a quiet room where I could take his things out of their pouch and untangle the chain of the Saint Christopher medal from the dog tag chains and arrange everything before his parents came in. I had twice before removed the items from the pouch to ensure they were all there—even though there was no chance anything could have fallen out. Each time, the two chains had been quite tangled. I didn't want to be fumbling around trying to untangle them in front of his parents. Our meeting, however, didn't go as expected.

I practically bumped into Chance's step-mom accidentally and our introductions began in the noisy hallway outside the gym. In short order I had met Chance's step-mom and father followed by his step-dad and, at last, his mom. I didn't know how to express to these people my sympathy for their loss and my gratitude for their sacrifice. Now, however, they were repeatedly thanking me for bringing their son home and for my service. I was humbled beyond words.

I told them that I had some of Chance's things and asked if we could try to find a quiet place. The five of us ended up in what appeared to be a computer lab—not what I had envisioned for this occasion.

After we had arranged five chairs around a small table, I told them about our trip. I told them how, at every step, Chance was treated with respect, dignity, and honor. I told them about the staff at Dover and all the folks at Northwest Airlines. I tried to convey how the entire Nation, from Dover to Philadelphia, to Minneapolis, to Billings, and Riverton expressed grief and sympathy over their loss.

Finally, it was time to open the pouch. The first item I happened to pull out was Chance's large watch. It was still set to Baghdad time. Next were the lanyard and the wooden cross. Then the dog tags and the Saint Christopher medal. This time the chains were not tangled. Once all of his items were laid out on the table, I told his mom that I had one other item to give them. I retrieved the flight attendant's crucifix from my pocket and told its story. I set that on the table and excused myself. When I next saw Chance's mom, she was wearing the crucifix on her lapel.

By 1400 most of the seats on the gym floor were filled and people were finding seats in the fixed bleachers high above the gym floor. There were a surprising number of people in military uniform. Many Marines had come up from Salt Lake City. Men from various VFW posts and the Marine Corps League occupied multiple rows of folding chairs. We all stood as Chance's family took their seats in the front.

It turned out that Chance's sister, a Petty Officer in the Navy, worked for a Rear Admiral—the Chief of Naval Intelligence—at the Pentagon. The Admiral had brought many of the sailors on his staff with him to Dubois to pay respects to Chance and support his sister. After a few songs and some words from a Navy Chaplain, the Admiral took the microphone and told us how Chance had died.

Chance was an artillery cannoneer and his unit was acting as provisional military police outside of Baghdad. Chance had volunteered to man a .50-caliber machine gun in the turret of the leading vehicle in a convoy. The convoy came under intense fire but Chance stayed true to his post and returned fire with the big gun, covering the rest of the convoy, until he was fatally wounded.

Then the commander of the local VFW post read some of the letters Chance had written home. In letters to his mom he talked of the mosquitoes and the heat. In letters to his stepfather he told of the dangers of convoy operations and of receiving fire.

The service was a fitting tribute to this hero. When it was over, we stood as the casket was wheeled out with the family following. The casket was placed onto a horse-drawn carriage for the mile-long trip from the gym, down the main street, then up the steep hill to the cemetery. I stood alone and saluted as the carriage departed the high school. I found my car and joined Chance's convoy.

The town seemingly went from the gym to the street. All along the route, the people had lined the street and were waving small American flags. The flags that were otherwise posted were all at half-staff. For the last quarter mile up the hill, local boy scouts, spaced about twenty feet apart, all in uniform, held large flags. At the foot of the hill, I could look up and back and see the enormity of our procession. I wondered how many people would be at this funeral if it were in, say, Detroit or Los Angeles—probably not as many as were here in little Dubois, Wyoming.

The carriage stopped about fifteen yards from the grave and the military pall bearers and the family waited until the men of the VFW and Marine Corps league were formed up and school busses had arrived carrying many of the people from the procession route. Once the entire crowd was in place, the pall bearers came to attention and began to remove the casket from the caisson. As I had done all week, I came to attention and executed a slow ceremonial salute as Chance was being transferred from one mode of transport to another.

From Dover to Philadelphia; Philadelphia to Minneapolis; Minneapolis to Billings; Billings to Riverton; and Riverton to Dubois we had been together. Now, as I watched them carry him the final

15 yards, I was choking up. I felt that, as long as he was still moving, he was somehow still alive.

Then they put him down above his grave. He had stopped moving.

Although my mission had been officially complete once I turned him over to the funeral director at the Billings airport, it was his placement at his grave that really concluded it in my mind. Now, he was home to stay and I suddenly felt at once sad, relieved, and useless.

The chaplain said some words that I couldn't hear and two Marines removed the flag from the casket and slowly folded it for presentation to his mother. When the ceremony was over, Chance's father placed a ribbon from his service in Vietnam on Chance's casket. His mother approached the casket and took something from her blouse and put it on the casket. I later saw that it was the flight attendant's crucifix. Eventually friends of Chance's moved closer to the grave. A young man put a can of Copenhagen on the casket and many others left flowers.

Finally, we all went back to the gym for a reception. There was enough food to feed the entire population for a few days. In one corner of the gym there was a table set up with lots of pictures of Chance and some of his sports awards. People were continually approaching me and the other Marines to thank us for our service. Almost all of them had some story to tell about their connection to the military. About an hour into the reception, I had the impression that every man in Wyoming had, at one time or another, been in the service.

It seemed like every time I saw Chance's mom she was hugging a different well wisher. As time passed, I began to hear people laughing. We were starting to heal.

After a few hours at the gym, I went back to the hotel to change out of my dress blues. The local VFW post had invited everyone over to "celebrate Chance's life." The Post was on the other end of town from my hotel and the drive took less than two minutes. The crowd was somewhat smaller than what had been at the gym but the Post was packed.

Marines were playing pool at the two tables near the entrance and most of the VFW members were at the bar or around the tables in the bar area. The largest room in the Post was a banquet/dining/dancing area and it was now called "The Chance Phelps Room." Above the entry were two items: a large portrait of Chance in his dress blues and the Eagle, Globe, & Anchor. In one corner of the room there was another memorial to Chance. There were candles burning around another picture of him in his blues. On the table surrounding his photo were his Purple Heart citation and his Purple Heart medal. There was also a framed copy of an excerpt from the Congressional Record. This was an elegant tribute to Chance Phelps delivered on the floor of the United States House of Representatives by Congressman Scott McInnis of Colorado. Above it all was a television that was playing a photo montage of Chance's life from small boy to proud Marine.

I did not buy a drink that night. As had been happening all day, indeed all week, people were thanking me for my service and for bringing Chance home. Now, in addition to words and handshakes, they were thanking me with beer. I fell in with the men who had handled the horses and horse-drawn carriage. I learned that they had worked through the night to groom and prepare the horses for Chance's last ride. They were all very grateful that they were able to contribute.

After a while we all gathered in the Chance Phelps Room for the formal dedication. The Post commander told us of how Chance had been so looking forward to becoming a Life Member of the VFW. Now, in the Chance Phelps Room of the Dubois, Wyoming Post, he would be an eternal member. We all raised our beers and the Chance Phelps Room was christened.

Later, as I was walking toward the pool tables, a Staff Sergeant from the Reserve unit in Salt Lake grabbed me and said, "Sir, you gotta hear this." There were two other Marines with him and he told the younger one, a lance corporal, to tell me his story. The staff sergeant said the lance corporal was normally too shy and modest to tell it but now he'd had enough beer to overcome his usual tendencies.

As the lance corporal started to talk, an older man joined our circle. He wore a baseball cap that indicated he had been with the 1st Marine Division in Korea. Earlier in the evening, he had told me about one of his former commanding officers: a Colonel Puller.

So, there I was, standing in a circle with three Marines recently returned from fighting with the 1st Marine Division in Iraq and one not so recently returned from fighting with the 1st Marine Division in Korea. I, who had fought with the 1st Marine Division in Kuwait, was about to gain a new insight into our Corps.

The young lance corporal began to tell us his story. At that moment, in this circle of current and former Marines, the differences in our ages and ranks dissipated—we were all simply Marines.

His squad had been on a patrol through a city street. They had taken small-arms fire and had literally dodged an RPG round that had sailed between two Marines. At one point they received fire from behind a wall and had neutralized the sniper with a SMAW round. The back blast of the SMAW, however, kicked up a substantial rock that hammered the lance corporal in the thigh; only missing his groin because he had reflexively turned his body sideways at the shot.

Their squad had suffered some wounded and was receiving more sniper fire when suddenly he was hit in the head by an AK-47 round. I was stunned as he told us how he felt like a baseball bat had been slammed into his head. He had spun around and fell unconscious. When he came to, he had a severe scalp wound but his Kevlar helmet had saved his life. He continued with his unit for a few days before realizing he was suffering the effects of a severe concussion.

As I stood there in the circle with the old man and the other Marines, the staff sergeant finished the story. He told of how this lance corporal had begged and pleaded with the Battalion surgeon to let him stay with his unit. In the end, the doctor said there was just no way—he had suffered a severe and traumatic head wound and would have to be medevaced.

The Marine Corps is a special fraternity. There are moments when we are reminded of this. Interestingly, those moments don't always happen at awards ceremonies or in dress blues at Birthday Balls. I have found, rather, that they occur at unexpected times and places: next to a loaded moving van at Camp Lejeune's base housing, in a dirty CP tent in northern Saudi Arabia, and in a smoky VFW post in western Wyoming.

After the story was done, the lance corporal stepped over to the old man, put his arm over the man's shoulder and told me that he, the Korean War vet, was his hero. The two of them stood there with their arms over each other's shoulders and we were all silent for a moment. When they let go, I told the lance corporal that there were recruits down on the yellow footprints tonight that would soon be learning his story.

I was finished drinking beer and telling stories. I found Chance's father and shook his hand one more time. Chance's mom had already left and I deeply regretted not being able to tell her goodbye.

I left Dubois in the morning before sunrise for my long drive back to Billings. It had been my honor to take Chance Phelps to his final post. Now he was on the high ground overlooking his town.

I miss him.

Regards,
Lt. Col. Strobl

★ ★ ★

Michael R. Strobl is an officer in the U. S. Marines. He lives and writes in Garrisonville, Virginia.

★ NOTHING EXCEPT A BATTLE

★ LOST CAN BE HALF SO

★ MELANCHOLY AS A BATTLE WON.

—ARTHUR WELLESLEY, DUKE OF WELLINGTON

PAT TILLMAN:
A SHORT LIFE

COMMANDER JOHN MCCAIN
(WITH MARK SALTER)

The sacrifice of the late Pat Tillman shows that courage and heroism are still alive and well in America.

★ ★ ★

He was quite a man, tough, honest, overachieving, intense, colorful, daring. A California kid who wore his blond hair long when short hair was in fashion and short when long hair was in fashion, and dressed routinely in shorts, T-shirts, and flip-flops. He came from a good family, who were as close as a family could be. His parents were strict, but fun and encouraging. He was raised to be brave, work hard, not to brag but to believe in himself. He married his high school sweetheart. He is remembered as the first one to help a friend in trouble, to stand up to a bully, to try to do the right thing. He thought for himself, and had, without doubt, the courage of his convictions.

He had played for the football team many of its fans argued was the best they had ever seen, San Jose's Leland High School Chargers. At the start of the second half of a game that had become a Leland rout, the Chargers' coach benched his starters and sent his subs in to finish off their overmatched opponents. Pat snuck back onto the field and returned a kickoff for a touchdown. That's one of the stories you always heard when someone was describing the larger-than-life legend that Pat Tillman has become

I'm a sports nut, and I was a Pat Tillman fan when he played for the Arizona State Sun Devils and the Arizona Cardinals. But I never met him. I wish I had. I wish I had known him all his life.

No one in Arizona expected much from him. At two hundred pounds, and under six feet, he was thought to be too small to play linebacker. He was offered Arizona State's last football scholarship in 1994, and the coach, although he was impressed by the young man's confidence and determination, never thought he would start a game, probably wouldn't even play at all unless the Sun Devils were ahead in a rout. He suggested to Pat that he red-shirt his freshman year. He thought that Pat should take the extra year to develop physically into a player who might have a shot at winning some playing time. Pat told him to forget it. He wasn't going to stay in college for five years, even if he sat on the bench his entire college career. He had other plans, and he was in a hurry. He completed the courses required for graduation in three and a half years, with a grade point average just a little short of perfect, and, to everyone's astonishment except his, was named the Pac-10 Conference Defensive Player of the Year. Thanks in large part to Pat Tillman's tough, smart, aggressive play, Arizona State had an 11-1 season his senior year and came within a whisker of being the national champions.

Still, everyone knew he was too small and too slow to play professional football. Everyone except Pat, and those who knew him well. He was chosen by the Arizona Cardinals in the seventh round of the 1998 NFL draft, the 226th player picked. Everyone thought he would sit on the bench, have some fun in the league as a kid who had no business in professional sports but would get to bask in the reflected glory and high living of marquee athletes for a couple of years, and would then, with his marketing degree from Arizona State, go do something else for a living. Two years later, as a strong safety for the Cardinals, hard-hitting Pat Tillman broke the team record for tackles, 224, each one of them bone-rattling. The next year, the Super Bowl champions, the St. Louis Rams, offered Pat a nine-million dollar contract. He turned them down. The Cardinals, who had given him a chance when others wouldn't, could afford to pay him less than half that generous sum. But they had his loyalty. And loyalty is something Pat Tillman took very seriously.

His agent, Frank Bauyer, didn't have many clients whose first priority was something other than making the biggest salary he could negotiate for them. But that was Pat Tillman, a different kind of man altogether from your typical professional athlete. He always had other priorities. He never charged a kid for his autograph. He never slowed down or tried to avoid fatigue or injury by giving less than a 100 percent effort on the field or in the rest of his life. He didn't hog the spotlight, but he wasn't shy. He just didn't believe he needed publicity to be a better football player or to feel better about himself. He loved challenges, and when he had accomplished something unexpected, he wanted a bigger challenge. He wanted to be the best football player he could, but much more important to him was becoming the best man he could.

He expressed his opinions on just about any subject, with the self-assuredness that marked him as an overachieving athlete. But he was smart enough, was wise enough, to keep an open mind, and let new experiences teach him, and information or a better argument persuade him. Honesty, like loyalty, was important to him.

In his senior year in high school, he got into trouble. When a friend of his was beaten up outside a local pizza parlor, Pat jumped in and beat the other kid to a pulp. He was arrested and sentenced to thirty days at a work farm for juvenile offenders. He thought his dreams of playing college football were over. But they weren't. Because he was a juvenile, the incident was erased from his record. No one outside his family and Leland High School need ever have found out about it. But he didn't hide it from anyone. He regretted the mistake. "I learned more from that one bad decision than all the good decisions I've ever made," he said. "It made me realize that stuff you do has repercussions. You can lose everything."

That's a good lesson to learn, and the earlier you learn it the better. But he didn't lose everything. He lost thirty days, and gained a little wisdom in exchange. When a reporter who knew nothing of the incident asked him if he had ever been arrested, he admitted that he had, and then, not because he had to, but because he felt he should, he described the offense and its repercussions in full.

I suppose September 11, 2001, is the day that young Americans will remember as I remember Pearl Harbor, a dividing line between the past and the present, unforgettable, and the day my father left for war to return years later a different man. Pat Tillman took the attacks on our country personally. Every American should have. He had been loyal to his football team, an honorable thing, but not the most important thing in someone's life. He knew Americans had much more important allegiances that we must live up to, and he intended to live up to his. He told a reporter the day after the attacks that he had relatives who had fought in America's previous wars, and he worried that, "I really haven't done a damn thing as far as laying myself on the line like that. . . . I have a lot of respect for those who have and what the flag stands for."

Our country's security doesn't depend on the heroism of every citizen. Nor does our individual happiness depend upon proving ourselves heroic. But we all have to be worthy of the sacrifices made on our behalf. We have to love our freedom, not just for the ease or material benefits it provides, not just for the autonomy it guarantees us, but for the goodness it makes possible. We have to love it so much we won't let it be constrained by fear or selfishness. We have to love it as much, even if not as heroically, as Pat Tillman loved it.

A few months after September 11, Pat Tillman told his agent he should concentrate on negotiating new contracts for his other clients, because he might have different plans. He married Marie Ugenti, the only girl he had ever loved, and spent a two-week honeymoon in Bora-Bora. I once saw a picture of them taken at their wedding reception. Pat was laying his head on his beautiful wife's lap, as happy as any man can be. It almost hurt to look at it. So young, so beautiful, so happy, at the beginning of what would surely have been a long and happy marriage. Not many people will ever have all the blessings Pat Tillman enjoyed on that fine May day when he married his one true love. Wealthy, famous, loved, and happy. It was a lot to put at risk. But he did risk it, all of it, because he knew he had obligations that could not be ignored without feeling ashamed of himself.

He and his brother, Kevin, a minor league baseball player who played his sport with as much courage and fierce determination as Pat played football, had been talking about their responsibilities to their country after we had been attacked. They decided that they should enlist in the military, and help defend the rest of us from the bin Ladens of the world. They decided they would become Army Rangers, an elite, special force reserved for some of the toughest, hardest combat assignments.

Pat walked into his coach's office just after he returned from his honeymoon and told him that he was going to leave football and his $3.9 million salary to join the army. His coach, knowing that his star defensive player was an exceptional man, wasn't particularly surprised by the decision. He was proud of him, and thankful for the

privilege of having coached the best man he had ever met in football. Then Pat and Kevin drove to Denver, Colorado, where they
hoped no one would notice them as they walked into a recruiter's
office, and enlisted in the United States Army.

They intentionally refused to talk about their decision. They
shunned all publicity. They refused all requests for interviews. They
didn't believe their decision was any more patriotic than the decisions of the less famous, less fortunate Americans who loved our
country enough to volunteer to defend us in a time of peril. They
didn't think they were better than any other soldier. And they were
right. They were special, but no more special than the Americans
they served with. But their modesty, as much as their sacrifice,
taught us the first lesson of patriotism. Patriotism is a lot more than
flag waving or singing the anthem at ball games. Patriotism is the
recognition that each of us is just one small part of a cause that is
greater than ourselves, one small part, but a part we are honor
bound to play. America is dedicated to the proposition that all men
are created equal, and have an equal right to freedom and justice.
That is our cause: to prove the truth of that proposition. And that
cause is far more important than the ambitions and desires of any
individual. To understand that truth is to be a true citizen of a great
republic, a true citizen like Pat and Kevin Tillman.

Pat and Kevin were as close as brothers could be, "tighter than
you could ever possibly know," a family friend observed. They cared
about the same things, each other, their family, their honor, their
country, and their responsibilities. They cared about being good
men. So they left for Ft. Benning, Georgia, and the hard training of
Army Rangers, stood out in their new profession as they had stood
out in every other endeavor they had undertaken, and then they
went to war.

They served in the same platoon, first in Iraq, where they distinguished themselves, and then in Afghanistan, where they joined

the hunt for Osama bin Laden. In between tours they came home to rest and train.

Their Ranger battalion's home base was Ft. Lewis in Washington State. The Cardinals' coach, Dave McGinnis, got in touch with Pat and asked him to come see the team when they played the Seattle Seahawks shortly before the Tillmans would leave for Afghanistan. Pat agreed, but insisted that he greet his teammates just as a friend, and not as somebody special who had come to lecture them on their duty to God and country. Pat walked into the locker room that Sunday and the Cardinals crowded around him, showing him their respect and thanking him. The undersize strong safety was, as he had often been in the past, the biggest man in the room.

He was happy to be in their company again but wouldn't talk about why he had given up the rewarding life of a professional football player for the $18,000 salary of an Army Ranger. Nor would he regale his teammates with combat stories or accept any tribute for his sacrifice. He had his reasons for serving, but he kept them to himself. He wished them luck, thanked his coach for the invitation, and left by a side door so no one would notice that Corporal Pat Tillman had come back to football, if just for a moment.

Combat veterans often refer to the "fog of war," because warfare, even today in this high-tech, precision-guided age, is inherently confusing. In Afghanistan it can be especially confusing. Dry and dusty, mountainous, where ambushes are easy to conceal and difficult to escape, where civilians can be hard to distinguish from enemies, it is an ancient killing ground where invading armies for centuries have been brought to grief by Afghans bred from birth to fight. Bad things can happen in the fog that make the losses incurred in war all the harder to bear, harder to forget, harder to forgive.

Something terrible happened in the early evening of April 29, 2004, on a mountain road near an Afghan village called Sperah, twenty-five miles from the nearest American base. As dusk dissolved into night, it was even harder to see what a soldier needed to see than it had been in the sun-blazed afternoon. The army got the story wrong at first. I don't know if they withheld the facts intentionally, but they surely waited inexcusably long before they informed Pat Tillman's family of how he had lost his life on that mountainside. Most of the facts are known now, and yet it still confuses those of us who did not see what happened with our own eyes. In truth, even some who witnessed the event are confused about how it occurred and why.

Suffice it to say that Pat Tillman died as he had lived, bravely, in the service of his country. His unit was looking for Taliban and al Qaeda fighters. They were divided, and separated at a distance that made it hard for the Rangers in each squad to see one another. The sound of gunfire, real or mistaken, caused the Rangers to believe they were under attack. Someone in the squad behind Pat Tillman mistook Pat and his squad for the enemy, and began to fire at them. Pat was killed.

That is an abrupt and colorless account of a good man's death. The details are easy enough to find if you're interested, but the fog of war, and this tragic, terrible mistake are hard things to comprehend even if you have all the facts. But the precise manner in which he lost his life makes him no less heroic. Soldiers go to war knowing they might lose everything. Pat Tillman knew he might lose everything. That he risked it anyway when no one expected him to made him a great man.

Kevin brought his brother's body home to California and his heartbroken family. His family, his friends, and his country wish they could have him back. We can only remember him as someone to admire, someone to emulate if we have his courage and decency and patriotism. I have used his life as an example of patriotism that I admire and encourage others to admire. I doubt he would approve. He didn't brag or, I suppose, like to hear others brag about him. So how should we remember him?

When he played for Arizona State, Pat used to like to climb one of the two-hundred-foot light towers at the stadium, and stay up there for some time contemplating what his future would be, what kind of man he would become. I think I'll remember him climbing down from the tower with the right answers to his questions.

★ ★ ★

John McCain, U.S. Senator from Arizona, lives and writes from his Arizona and Washington, D.C. homes. All of his books have become best-sellers.

ACKNOWLEDGMENTS

Introduction: "The Fascination of War," by Joseph Leininger Wheeler. Copyright © 2006. Printed by permission of the author.

"The Flying Madman," by Joseph V. Mizrahi. Published in Phil Hirsch's *Fighting Eagles*, (New York: Pyramid Books, 1961). If anyone can provide knowledge of earliest publication source of this old story, or the whereabouts of the author's next of kin, please send to Joe Wheeler (P.O. Box 1246, Conifer, CO 80433).

"The Yanks Go Through," by Williams Slavens McNutt. Published in *Collier's*, October 5, 1918. Text owned by Joe Wheeler.

"Carrier Pigeons Are Real Heroes," author unknown. Published in *The Youth's Instructor*, April 20, 1926. Reprinted by permission of Joe Wheeler (P.O. Box 1246, Conifer, CO 80433) and Review and Herald Publishing Association, Hagerstown, MD.

"How the British Sank the *Scharnhorst*," by C. S. Forester. Reprinted from The Saturday Evening Post magazine, Copyright © 1944 Saturday Evening Post Society. Reprinted with permission, www.saturdayeveningpost.com.

"Give Us This Day," by Sergeant Sidney Stewart. Originally published in Stewart's *Give Us This Day* (New York: W.W. Norton, 1957). Reprinted by permission of W. W. Norton and The Balkin Agency.

"Doolittle's Raid on Tokyo," by Martin Caidin. Published in Phil Hirsch's *Fighting Eagles* (New York: Pyramid Books, 1961). If anyone can provide knowledge of Martin Caidin's next of kin or earliest publication source of this story, please send to Joe Wheeler (P.O. Box 1246, Conifer, CO 80433).

"Voyage to Faith," by Thomas Fleming, is reprinted with permission of *Guideposts* magazine. Copyright © 1995 by Guideposts, Carmel, New York 10512. All rights reserved.

"The Lost Fortress," by Ernie Pyle. Published in *Here Is Your War* (New York: Henry Holt, 1944). Reprinted by permission of Scripps Howard Foundation.

"The Dresden Inferno," by Anne Wahle, as told to Roul Tunley. Published in *Ordeal by Fire* (New York: Dell Publishing Company, 1967). If anyone can provide knowledge of author or author's next of kin, please send to Joe Wheeler (P.O. Box 1246, Conifer, CO 80433).

"Beyond the River Kwai," by Eric Lomax. Published in *Guideposts*, October 1996. From *The Railway Man: a POWs Searing Account of War, Brutality and Forgiveness*, by Eric Lomax. Copyright © 1995 by Eric Lomax. Used by permission of W. W. Norton Company, Inc.

"A New Skipper for Charlie Company," by Ken Jones. Published in Jones's *I Was There* (New York: Lion Books, 1953). If anyone can provide knowledge of earliest publication source of this story, or the whereabouts of the author or the author's next of kin, please send to Joe Wheeler (P.O. Box 1246, Conifer, CO 80433).

"Mercy Flight," by Lt. Alan D. Fredericks and Michael Gladyn. Published in Phil Hirsch's *Fighting Eagles* (New York: Pyramid Books, 1961). If anyone can provide knowledge of earliest publication source of this story, or the whereabouts of the author or the author's next of kin please send to Joe Wheeler (P.O. Box 1246, Conifer, CO 80433).

"Mike's Flag," by Commander John McCain and Mark Salter. Published in McCain's *Faith of My Fathers*. Copyright © 1999. Reprinted by permission of Random House, Inc.

"Taking Chance," by Lt. Col. Michael R. Strobl, U.S.M.C. Copyright © 2004. Reprinted by permission of the author.

"Pat Tillman: a Short Life," by Commander John McCain and Mark Salter. Published in McCain's *Character Is Destiny*. Copyright © 2005. Reprinted by permission of Random House, Inc.